THE
DILBERT™
PRINCIPLE

THE
DILBERT™
PRINCIPLE

A Cubicle's-Eye
View of Bosses, Meetings,
Management Fads &
Other Workplace Afflictions

SCOTT ADAMS

HarperBusiness
A Division of HarperCollinsPublishers

A hardcover edition of this book was published in 1996 by HarperBusiness, a division of HarperCollins Publishers.

First paperback edition published 1997.

Designed by Caitlin Daniels

The Library of Congress has catalogued the hardcover edition as follows:

Adams, Scott, 1957–
    The Dilbert principle : a cubicle's-eye view of bosses, meetings, management fads & other workplace afflictions / Scott Adams.
        p.   cm.
    ISBN 0-88730-787-6
    1. Management.   2. Office politics.   3. Personnel management.   I. Title.
HD31.A294   1996
650.1'3—dc20   96-388

ISBN 0-88730-858-9 (pbk.)

97 98 99 00 01 ❖/RRD 10 9 8 7 6 5 4 3 2 1

For Pam

CONTENTS

BIG OPENING

These days it seems like any idiot with a laptop computer can churn out a business book and make a few bucks. That's certainly what I'm hoping. It would be a real letdown if the trend changed before this masterpiece goes to print.

As some of you may know, my main profession is cartooning. It's a challenge for a cartoonist to write a whole book. Cartoonists are trained to be brief. Everything I've learned in my entire life can be boiled down to a dozen bullet points, several of which I've already forgotten.

You'd feel kinda perturbed if you bought a big thick book and all it had in it was a dozen bullet points, particularly if several of them seemed to be "filler." So my "plan for excellence" is to repeat myself often to take up some page space. In marketing terms, this is called "adding value." And for your reading pleasure I will include many colorful but unnecessary metaphors. In fact, the metaphors in this book are more useless than a weasel in a cardboard shirt.°

°I can't promise that the rest will be that good.

THE
DILBERT™
PRINCIPLE

WHY IS BUSINESS SO ABSURD?

Most of the themes in my comic strip "Dilbert" involve workplace situations. I routinely include bizarre and unworldly elements such as sadistic talking animals, troll-like accountants, and employees turning into dishrags after the life-force has been drained from their bodies. And yet the comment I hear most often is:

> "That's just like my company."

No matter how absurd I try to make the comic strip I can't stay ahead of what people are experiencing in their own workplaces. Some examples for the so-called real world include:

- A major technology company simultaneously rolled out two new programs: (1) a random drug testing program, and (2) an "Individual Dignity Enhancement" program.

- A company purchased laptop computers for employees to use while traveling. Fearing they might be stolen, the managers came up with a clever solution: permanently attach the laptop computers to the employees' desks.

- A freight company reorganized to define roles and clarify goals. Management decided to communicate the changes by ordering each department to build floats for a "Quality Parade."

- A manager at a telecommunications company wanted to reinforce the "team" concept in his department. He held a meeting to tell the assembled "team" that henceforth he will carry a baseball bat with him at all times and each team member will carry a baseball while at work. Some team members found a way to hang the baseball around their necks so they don't have to carry it. Others fantasized about wrestling the bat away from the manager and using it.

- A company decided that instead of raises it will give bonuses if five of seven company goals are met. At the end of the year the employees are informed that they have met only four of seven goals, so no bonuses. One of the goals they missed was "employee morale."

Thousands of people have told me workplace stories (mostly through e-mail) that are even more absurd than the examples above. When I first started hearing these stories I was puzzled, but after careful analysis I have developed a sophisticated theory to explain the existence of this bizarre workplace behavior: People are idiots.

Including me. Everyone is an idiot, not just the people with low SAT scores. The only differences among us is that we're idiots about different things at different times. No matter how smart you are, you spend much of your day being an idiot. That's the central premise of this scholarly work.

MANDATORY SELF-DEPRECATION

I proudly include myself in the idiot category. Idiocy in the modern age isn't an all-encompassing, twenty-four-hour situation for most people. It's a condition that everybody slips into many times a day. Life is just too complicated to be smart all the time.

The other day I brought my pager to the repair center because it wouldn't work after I changed the battery. The repairman took the pager out of my hand, flipped open the battery door, turned the battery around, and handed the now functional pager back to me in one well-practiced motion. This took much of the joy out of my righteous indignation over the quality of their product. But the repairman seemed quite amused. And so did every other customer in the lobby.

On that day, in that situation, I was a complete idiot. Yet somehow I managed to operate a motor vehicle to the repair shop and back. It is a wondrous human characteristic to be able to slip into and out of idiocy many times a day without noticing the change or accidentally killing innocent bystanders in the process.

MY QUALIFICATIONS

Now that I've admitted that I can't replace the battery in my pager, you might wonder what makes me think I'm qualified to write this important book. I think you'll be impressed at my depth of experience and accomplishment:

1. I convinced a company to publish this book. That might not seem like much, but it's more than you did today. And it wasn't easy. I had to have lunch with people I didn't even know.

2. I worked in a cubicle for seventeen years. Most business books are written by consultants and professors who haven't spent much time in a cubicle. That's like writing a firsthand account of the experience of the Donner party based on the fact that you've eaten beef jerky. Me, I've gnawed an ankle or two.

3. I'm a trained hypnotist. Years ago I took a class to learn how to hypnotize people. As a byproduct of this training I learned that people are mindless, irrational, easily manipulated dolts. (I think I paid $500 to learn that.) And it's not just the so-called good subjects—it's everybody. It's how our brains are wired. You make up your mind first and then you rationalize it second. But because of the odd mapping of your perceptions you're convinced beyond a doubt that your decisions are based on reason. They aren't.

Important scientists have done studies° proving that the area of the brain responsible for rational thought doesn't even activate

---

°They were important scientists, but not so important that I would remember their names and not so important that you'd care. But I'm sure it's true because I read it in a magazine.

until *after* you do something. You can confirm that fact using hypnosis, by giving a person an irrational post-hypnotic suggestion and asking later why the subject did what he did. He will insist it made sense at the time, employing a logic more tortured than Pavarotti at a Tiny Tim concert.

A hypnotist quickly develops a complete distrust for the connection between a person's reasons and his actions. The class fundamentally changed the way I look at the world.

4. Nobody believes statistics anyway. This is a huge time-saver for me as an author. It removes any guilt I might have about fabricating statistics. If you're a "normal" person, you tend to believe any studies that support your current views and ignore everything else. Therefore, any reference I might make to legitimate research is wasted. If we can agree on the futility of trying to sway you with legitimate research it will save us both a lot of trouble.

That doesn't mean I will ignore statistics. Far from it. Throughout this book I will make references to scientific studies. Of course, they'll all be total fabrications. But my versions will make better reading than legitimate research, and ultimately the impact is the same.

If you think about it, most of the studies you see in the media are either completely misleading or intentionally biased. This book is no different, except that I don't underestimate your intelligence. I mean, how could I?

THE ROLE OF INTELLIGENCE IN BUSINESS

I don't know why the economy works, but I'm sure it isn't because brilliant people are managing it. My guess is that if you sum up all the absurd activities of management, the idiocies somehow cancel out, thus producing cool things that you want to buy, such as Nerf balls and Snapple. Add the law of supply and demand to the mix and you've pretty much described the whole theory of economics.

Ninety percent of all new business ventures fail. Apparently, ten percent of the time you get lucky, and that's enough to support a modern economy. I'm betting that's what separates us from the animals; animals are lucky only nine percent of the time. I suspect this is true because I play strip poker with my cats and they rarely win. In fact, it's gotten to the point where they run like cowards at the sound of my electric shaver.

The world has become so complicated that we're all bluffing our way through the business day, hoping we're not unmasked for the boobs that we really are. I see the world as a massively absurd endeavor, populated by people who struggle every minute to rationalize the silly things they do.

It's not the business world that brings out our idiocy, but it might be the place where we notice it the most. In our personal lives we tolerate bizarre behavior. It even seems normal. (If you don't believe me, take a look at your family members.) But at work we think everyone should be guided by logic and rational thinking. Any absurdity in a business setting stands out like a dead nun in a snowbank.° I'm convinced that the workplace doesn't contain more absurdity than everyday life, but the absurdity is definitely more noticeable.

I find great humor in the fact that we ever take ourselves seriously. We rarely recognize our own idiocies, yet we can clearly identify the idiocies of others. That's the central tension of business:

> We expect others to act rationally even though we are irrational.

It's useless to expect rational behavior from the people you work with, or anybody else for that matter. If you can come to peace with the fact that you're surrounded by idiots, you'll realize that resistance is futile, your tension will dissipate, and you can sit back and have a good laugh at the expense of others. This can be a very healthy book.

THE EVOLUTION OF IDIOTS

Scientists believe that humans are the grand result of billions of years of evolution. I can't explain the entire theory of evolution here, but it can be summarized this way.

Theory of Evolution (Summary)

First, there were some amoebas. Deviant amoebas adapted better to the environment, thus becoming monkeys. Then came Total Quality Management.

I'm leaving out some details, but the theory itself also has a few holes that are best left unquestioned.

°If it bothers you to think of a dead nun, imagine that she's only badly wounded and she'll recover.

Anyway, it took us many years to get to this lofty level of evolution. That leisurely pace of change was okay because there wasn't much to do except sit around and hope you didn't get eaten by wild pigs. Then somebody fell on a sharp stick and the spear was invented. That's when the trouble started.

I wasn't there, but I'm willing to bet that some people said the spear would never replace fingernails as the fighting tool of choice. The naysayers probably hurled bad names at the spear-users—names like "moog" and "blinth." (This was before the merchant marines had been created, so swearing wasn't very good yet.)

But "diversity" was not celebrated back then, and I expect the "Say No to Spear" people finally got the "point" if you catch my drift.

The good thing about a spear is that almost everybody could understand it. It had basically one feature: the pointy end. Our brains were fully equipped for this level of complexity. And not just the brains of the intelligentsia either—the common man could find his way around a spear too. Life was good, save for the occasional plague and the fact that the average life expectancy was seven . . . and the fact that you'd be praying for death after the age of four. But almost nobody complained about how confusing the spears were.

Suddenly (in evolutionary terms) some deviant went and built the printing press. It was a slippery slope after that. Two blinks later and we're switching batteries in our laptop computers while streaking through the sky in shiny metal objects in which soft drinks and peanuts are served.

I blame sex and paper for most of our current problems. Here's my logic: Only one person in a million is smart enough to invent a printing press. So when society consisted of only a few hundred apelike people living in caves, the odds of one of them being a genius were fairly low. But people kept having sex, and with every moron added to the population, the odds of a deviant smarty-pants slipping through the genetic net got higher and higher. When you've got several million people running around having sex all willy-nilly,*

---

* If you haven't tried having sex "all willy-nilly" you really should.

the odds are fairly good that some pregnant ape-mom is going to squat in a field someday and pinch out a printing-press-making deviant.

Once we had printing presses, we were pretty much doomed. Because then, every time a new smart deviant came up with a good idea, it would get written down and shared. Every good idea could be built upon. Civilization exploded. Technology was born. The complexity of life increased geometrically. Everything got bigger and better.

Except our brains.

All the technology that surrounds us, all the management theories, the economic models that predict and guide our behavior, the science that helps us live to eighty—it's all created by a tiny percentage of deviant smart people. The rest of us are treading water as fast as we can. The world is too complex for us. Evolution didn't keep up. Thanks to the printing press, the deviant smart people managed to capture their genius and communicate it without having to pass it on genetically. Evolution was short-circuited. We got knowledge and technology before we got intelligence.

We're a planet of nearly six billion ninnies living in a civilization that was designed by a few thousand amazingly smart deviants.

True Example

Kodak introduced a single-use camera called the Weekender. Customers have called the support line to ask if it's okay to use it during the week.

The rest of this book builds on my theory that we're all idiots. I'm sure there are other plausible explanations for why business seems so absurd but I can't think of any. If I do, I'll write another book for you. I promise I won't stop searching for an answer until you run out of money.

1

THE DILBERT PRINCIPLE*

I use a lot of "bad boss" themes in my syndicated cartoon strip "Dilbert." I'll never run out of material. I get at least two hundred e-mail messages a day, mostly from people who are complaining about their own clueless managers. Here are some of my favorite stories, all allegedly true:

- A vice president insists that the company's new battery-powered product be equipped with a light that comes on to tell you when the power is off.

*This article originally appeared in the *Wall Street Journal* on May 22, 1995. It got a huge response and led to the creation of this book.

- An employee suggests setting priorities so the company will know how to apply its limited resources. The manager's response: "Why can't we concentrate our resources across the board?"

- A manager wants to find and fix software bugs more quickly. He offers an incentive plan: $20 for each bug the Quality Assurance people find and $20 for each bug the programmers fix. (These are the same programmers who create the bugs.) Result: An underground economy in "bugs" springs up instantly. The plan is rethought after one employee nets $1,700 the first week.

Stories like these prompted me to do the first annual Dilbert Survey to find out what management practices were most annoying to employees. The choices included the usual suspects: Quality, Empowerment, Reengineering, and the like. But the number-one vote-getter in this highly unscientific survey was "Idiots Promoted to Management."

This seemed like a subtle change from the old concept by which capable workers were promoted until they reached their level of incompetence—best described as the "Peter Principle." Now, apparently, the incompetent workers are promoted directly to management without ever passing through the temporary competence stage.

When I entered the workforce in 1979, the Peter Principle described management pretty well. Now I think we'd all like to return to those Golden Years when you had a boss who was once good at something.

I get all nostalgic when I think about it. Back then, we all had hopes of being promoted beyond our levels of competence. Every worker had a shot at someday personally navigating the company into the tar pits while reaping large bonuses and stock options. It was a time when inflation meant everybody got an annual raise; a time when we freely admitted that the customers didn't matter. It was a time of joy.

We didn't appreciate it then, but the much underrated Peter Principle always provided us with a boss who understood what we did for a living. Granted, he made consistently bad decisions—after all, he had no management skills. But at least they were the informed decisions of a seasoned veteran from the trenches.

Example

Boss: "When I had your job I could drive a three-inch rod through a metal casing with one motion. If you're late again I'll do the same thing to your head."

Nitpickers found lots of problems with the Peter Principle, but on the whole it worked. Lately, however, the Peter Principle has given way to the "Dilbert Principle." The basic concept of the Dilbert Principle is that the most ineffective workers are systematically moved to the place where they can do the least damage: management.

This has not proved to be the winning strategy that you might think.

Maybe we should learn something from nature. In the wild, the weakest moose is hunted down and killed by dingo dogs, thus ensuring survival of the fittest. This is a harsh system—especially for the dingo dogs who have to fly all the way from Australia. But nature's process is a good one; everybody agrees, except perhaps for the dingo dogs and the moose in question . . . and the flight attendants. But the point is that we'd all be better off if the least competent managers were being eaten by dingo dogs instead of writing Mission Statements.

It seems as if we've turned nature's rules upside down. We systematically identify and promote the people who have the least skills. The usual business rationalization for promoting idiots (the Dilbert Principle in a nutshell) is something along the lines of "Well, he can't write code, he can't design a network, and he doesn't have any sales skill. But he has *very* good hair . . . "

If nature started organizing itself like a modern business, you'd see, for example, a band of mountain gorillas led by an "alpha" squirrel. And it wouldn't be the most skilled squirrel; it would be the squirrel nobody wanted to hang around with.

I can see the other squirrels gathered around an old stump saying stuff like "If I hear him say, 'I like nuts' one more time, I'm going to kill him." The gorillas, overhearing this conversation, lumber down from the mist and promote the unpopular squirrel. The remaining squirrels are assigned to Quality Teams as punishment.

You may be wondering if you fit the description of a Dilbert Principle manager. Here's a little test:

1. Do you believe that anything you don't understand must be easy to do?

2. Do you feel the need to explain in great detail why "profit" is the difference between income and expense?

3. Do you think employees should schedule funerals only during holidays?

4. Are the following words a form of communication or gibberish:

    The Business Services Leadership Team will enhance the organization in order to continue on the journey toward a Market Facing Organization (MFO) model. To that end, we are consolidating the Object Management for Business Services into a cross strata team.

5. When people stare at you in disbelief do you repeat what you just said, only louder and more slowly?

Now give yourself one point for each question you answered with the letter "B." If your score is greater than zero, congratulations—there are stock options in your future.

(The language in question four is from an actual company memo.)

THE DILBERT PRINCIPLE ILLUSTRATED

I NEED TO PROMOTE ONE OF YOU TO THE DISTRICT MANAGER POSITION.
DILBERT, YOUR TECHNICAL KNOWLEDGE IS TOO VALUABLE TO LOSE.
DITTO FOR ALICE. NEITHER OF YOU CAN BE PROMOTED.
THE ONLY LOGICAL CHOICE IS TO PROMOTE AL BECAUSE HE HAS NO VALUABLE KNOWLEDGE.
AL??! A DIRECTOR??! HE DOESN'T KNOW WHAT DAY OF THE WEEK IT IS!!
THEY'RE JUST GRUMPY BECAUSE IT'S MONDAY.
IT'S THURSDAY.

I MADE A FEW CHANGES TO THE DESIGN.
WE'LL HAVE TO WORK AROUND THE CLOCK FOR MONTHS TO MAKE THESE CHANGES!!
WORK SMARTER, NOT HARDER.
YOU'RE TRYING TO VIOLATE THE LAWS OF PHYSICS!
RULES WERE MADE TO BE BROKEN.
THIS DESIGN WOULD CREATE ENOUGH RADIATION TO INSTANTLY KILL THE USER!!
BE SURE TO MENTION THAT IN THE DOCUMENTATION.
LET'S WORK SMARTER NOT HARDER.
I THINK WE FOUND THE ONLY "BETA" TESTER WE'LL NEED.

I JUST HEARD THAT LIGHT TRAVELS FASTER THAN SOUND.
I'M WONDERING IF I SHOULD SHOUT WHEN I SPEAK, JUST SO MY LIPS APPEAR TO SYNC-UP WITH MY WORDS.
A LITTLE KNOWLEDGE CAN BE A RIDICULOUS THING.
HE PROBABLY HASN'T HEARD ME YET.

2

HUMILIATION

Employee morale is a risky thing. Happy employees will work harder without asking for extra pay. But if they get too happy, endorphins kick in, egos expand, and everybody starts whining about the fact that with their current pay they'll have to live in a dumpster after retirement.

The best balance of morale for employee productivity can be described this way: happy, but with low self-esteem.

You can test your own level of employee happiness with this test. If you laugh out loud at any of the "office witticisms" shown here, then you are happy in exactly the right amount to be productive:

HAPPINESS PRODUCTIVITY TEST

Below are several witticisms encountered in your office every day. How many do you find irresistibly funny?

1. "Are you working hard or hardly working?"

2. "Are you holding up the wall?"

3. "You look different today!" (said to someone at a borrowed desk)

4. "It's not my day to watch Bob."

5. "Not bad for a Wednesday!"

If you laughed at any of the five witticisms, you have the proper Dopey-from-the-Seven-Dwarfs kind of happy that spells productivity. But if during this test you suddenly got a mental image of a co-worker you'd like to bludgeon with a speakerphone, then you might have too much self-esteem to be productive.

THE SOLUTION: HUMILIATION

Over the years, businesses have developed a broad range of techniques that bring employees' self-esteem back into the "productive zone" without sacrificing happiness. This chapter discusses the most important humiliation techniques.

- Cubicles

- Hoteling

- Furniture

- Dress clothes

- Employee Recognition Programs

- Undervaluing employee contributions

- Making them wait

CUBICLES

Cubicles—sometimes called "work spaces" or "pods"—serve as a constant reminder of the employee's marginal value to the company. I've never seen a brochure from a cubicle manufacturer, but I think it would look something like this:

The Cubicle 6000™ Series

Think of The Cubicle 6000™ as a lifestyle, not just a big box to keep your crap in one place!!

We used nature as our guide when we designed The Cubicle 6000™. Every unit has the unmistakable motivational feel of the four most inspiring locations on earth:

VEAL-FATTENING PEN:

Imagine the security that those lucky young cows feel, snug in their individual living units, without a care in the world. The reaffirming message is "Live for today!"

CARDBOARD BOX:

It's the same architecture that has transported the possessions of successful people for hundreds of years!

BABY'S PLAYPEN:

A reminder of the exuberance of youth and the thrill of being held captive by strange people who speak gibberish and punish you for reasons you don't understand!

PRISON CELL:

We've "captured" the carefree feeling of a convict serving twenty to life. Experience the security that was previously available only in the penal system!

And look at these features!!

- Open top so you'll never miss a surrounding noise.

- Small size so you can enjoy the odors of your co-workers.

- No annoying windows.

- Available in battleship gray or feces brown.

- Movable— discover the thrill of frequent office shuffling.

- Coat hanger (only available on the Admiral Series).

WE'VE GOT A LOT OF EMPTY CUBICLES BECAUSE OF DOWNSIZING.
S. Adams E-mail: SCOTTADAMS@AOL.COM
I HIRED THE DOGBERT CONSTRUCTION COMPANY TO CONVERT PART OF THE OFFICE INTO PRISON CELLS
WHICH WE'LL LEASE TO THE STATE.
4-24 © 1995 United Feature Syndicate, Inc. (NYC)
SOUNDS LIKE A BIG JOB.
NAH. A LITTLE PAINT, NEW CARPET AND WE'RE THERE.

I DON'T THINK IT'S FAIR TO PUT CONVICTS IN OUR SPARE CUBICLES.
S. Adams E-mail: SCOTTADAMS@AOL.COM
DON'T BE SUCH A BIGOT. THESE PEOPLE HAVE MADE ONE LITTLE MISTAKE. OTHERWISE, THEY'RE JUST LIKE EMPLOYEES.
4-25 © 1995 United Feature Syndicate, Inc. (NYC)
I THINK THERE ARE A FEW DIFFERENCES!
YEAH, THEIR HEALTH PLAN IS BETTER.

HEY, BUDDY, WHAT ARE YOU IN FOR?
S. Adams E-mail: SCOTTADAMS@AOL.COM
UNLIKE YOURSELF, I AM NOT A PRISONER HERE. I CHOOSE TO WORK HERE OF MY OWN FREE WILL!
4-26 © 1995 United Feature Syndicate, Inc. (NYC)
GREAT... I'M IN THE FREAK SECTION.
I LIKE TO WORK.

EFFECTIVE IMMEDIATELY, WE WILL NO LONGER USE OUR SPARE CUBICLES TO HOUSE CONVICTS.
S. Adams E-mail: SCOTTADAMS@AOL.COM
YES!!! OUR OPINIONS MATTERED!
ACTUALLY, IT'S BECAUSE THE PRISONERS COMPLAINED.
4-27 © 1995 United Feature Syndicate, Inc. (NYC)
I WONDER WHAT HE PLANS TO DO WITH THE SPARE CUBICLES NOW.

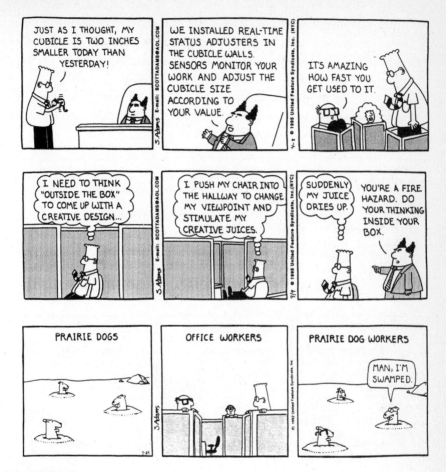

HOTELING

The only drawback to the cubicle-oriented office is that some employees develop a sense of "home" in their little patch of real estate. Soon, pride of ownership sets in, then self-esteem, and *poof*—good-bye productivity.

But thanks to the new concept of "hoteling," this risk can be eliminated. Hoteling is a system by which cubicles are assigned to the employees as they show up each day. Nobody gets a permanent work space, and therefore no unproductive homey feelings develop.

Another advantage: Hoteling eliminates all physical evidence of the employee's association with the company. This takes the fuss out of down-sizing; the employee doesn't even have to clean out a desk. With hoteling, every employee has "one foot out the door" at all times.

Hoteling sends an important message to the employee: "Your employment is temporary. Keep your photos of your ugly family in the trunk of your car so we don't have to look at them."

FURNITURE

You're only as important as your furniture. And that's at peak levels of dignity. Often you're less important than your furniture. If you think about it, you can get fired but your furniture stays behind, gainfully employed at the company that didn't need *you* anymore.

It's no surprise that people invest a great deal of ego in their office furniture. Depending on your status in the company, your furniture sends one of these two messages:

"Ignore the worthless object sitting on this chair."

Or . . .

"*Worship me!!* Kneel before the mahogany shrine!"

Given a choice, you want furniture that sends that second message. Unfortunately, impressive furniture is available only at higher levels of management. Statistically speaking, the reader of this paragraph is not likely to be a member of senior management. So I'll skip that discussion.

Assuming you're not in senior management, you might be lucky to have a big ol' board that stretches the length of your cubicle and keeps the telephone from falling in your lap. Let's call it a "desk" for the sake of argument. This desklike arrangement is the perfect complement to the tiny chair that will be your home for seventy hours a week.

If you're a secretary, your chair probably has no armrests. That's okay; you weren't hired to rest your arms. You should be busy finding ways to prevent the professional staff from meeting with your boss. *That's* what you're getting paid to do, dammit.

But if you're not a secretary, you might be enjoying the luxury of armrests. Those armrests are essential for balance if you plan to nap in your cubicle. During my career at Pacific Bell I spent many blissful hours sound asleep in my cubicle, thanks to armrests. I always located my computer so my back faced the aisle when I looked at the screen. That way I could pull up a document, balance my arms on the armrests, close my eyes, and drift into Sugarland, all while looking like a dedicated employee. Sometimes the phone would ring, but I learned to screen it out. (The brain is an amazing thing!)

Despite being well-rested, sometimes even "Dopey Happy," I never achieved enough self-esteem at Pacific Bell to become cocky. My furniture did its job, providing just the right level of humility to maintain my fever-pitch of productivity.

E-mail From the Cubicle Trenches

As you can see from these examples, money is no object compared to the importance of keeping the employees in their proper place.

From: (name withheld)
To: scottadams@aol.com

Scott,

Now that we've reengineered, we have fewer managers than we have windows! Big problem, but we have a solution. We've erected five-foot-high partition walls in front of the windows, so that non-managers can sit there without offending the pecking order.

From: (name withheld)
To: scottadams@aol.com

Scott,

I thought you'd enjoy this:
Someone I know works at a government agency—they recently reorganized people in the Engineering Department and a lowly non-management type was put into the corner space of the work areas. Since the space had walls put up a year ago to accommodate a manager, they are actually hiring contractors to come in and have the walls taken out for the lowly nonmanager!

From: (name withheld)
To: scottadams@aol.com

Scott,

Recently, our office moved down the street. Around the same time, I was fortunate to be promoted to a new job.

As with all large companies, the allotment of cubicle and office space is associated with grade level (for example, if you are grade X, you get a sixty-four-square-foot cubicle; if you are grade Y, you get a one-hundred-square-foot office). Finally, after a few diligent years of corporate service, my grade level afforded me an office.

This is all well and good; however, my grade level did not specify nice, wooden office furniture. I still have many levels yet to go. Therefore, in an effort to reuse cubicles from the previous facility, the real estate arm of my company installed a cubicle within my office. Imagine for the moment how ridiculous this looks.

Now, the funny part is that the office I occupy has a window; however, it is completely blocked by the cubicle wall.

MY CHAIR IS BROKEN AND THE WAREHOUSE IS OUT OF "ENGINEER CHAIRS."
AND SINCE I'M ... YOU KNOW... EMPOWERED, I THOUGHT I MIGHT ORDER A "MANAGER CHAIR" FOR THE TIME BEING.
I'VE OVER-STEPPED MY AUTHORITY, HAVEN'T I?
NEXT YOU'LL WANT A SCREEN DOOR ON YOUR CUBICLE.
S.Adams E-Mail: SCOTTADAMS@AOL.COM
© 1993 United Feature Syndicate, Inc.
12-7

IF THE WAREHOUSE WON'T REPLACE MY BROKEN CHAIR, I'LL JUST TAKE ONE FROM SOMEBODY ELSE.
TECHNICALLY, IT'S NOT STEALING BECAUSE THE CHAIR BELONGS TO THE COMPANY EITHER WAY.
WHAT'S THE WORST THING THAT COULD HAPPEN?
HOLD THE ELEVATOR. ...OVER.
S.Adams E-Mail: SCOTTADAMS@AOL.COM
© 1993 United Feature Syndicate, Inc.
12-8

IT'S "PHIL, THE PRINCE OF INSUFFICIENT LIGHT"!
I SAW YOU TAKE THAT CHAIR.
I SUMMON ALL THE DEMONS AND TROLLS OF HECK TO COME FORTH AND PUNISH YOU NOW!!!
I'M ED, FROM ACCOUNTING. THE OTHERS ARE AT LUNCH.
S.Adams E-Mail: SCOTTADAMS@AOL.COM
© 1993 United Feature Syndicate, Inc.
12-9

WHAT'S THE PENALTY FOR STEALING A CHAIR??
YOU ARE SENTENCED TO SIT IN THE BREAK ROOM USED BY THE ACCOUNTING DEPARTMENT.
I LIKE TO TYPE THE NUMBER SIX.
CRIPES! THIS IS MY TUESDAY LUNCH BAG.
S.Adams E-Mail: SCOTTADAMS@AOL.COM
© 1993 United Feature Syndicate, Inc.
12-10

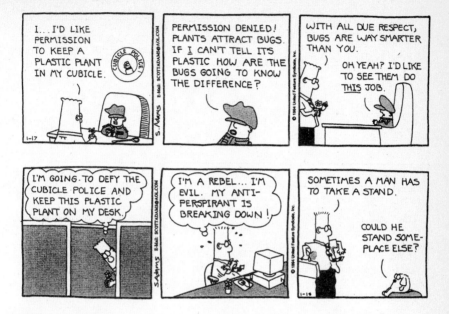

DRESS CLOTHES

Nothing is more adorable than one of those little organ-grinder monkeys with a tiny vest and a hat. That would be the official uniform at your company too if not for the fact it would be considered a "uniform" and there's no budget for that sort of thing.

Companies have discovered a low-cost method for making people dress in the same humiliating fashion as the monkey but without the expense of buying uniforms. The secret is to specify a style of acceptable dress that has the same symbolism as the monkey's outfit but allows some variety:

CLOTHING	SYMBOLISM
Necktie	Leash
Pantyhose	Leg irons; prisoner
Suit jacket	Penguin; incapable of flight
High heels	Masochism

CATBERT THE HR DIRECTOR
I THINK I'LL INVENT SOME ILLOGICAL POLICIES TO ANNOY EMPLOYEES.
S. Adams E-mail: SCOTTADAMS@AOL.COM
MY DIABOLICAL NEW DRESS CODE WILL MAKE THEM QUESTION THEIR OWN SANITY.
8/7 © 1995 United Feature Syndicate, Inc. (NYC)
... SO, CASUAL CLOTHES DON'T LOWER OUR STOCK VALUE... BUT ONLY IF WORN ON FRIDAYS... UNLESS SOMEBODY SEES US... GOT IT?
I THINK I'M INSANE.

I DON'T UNDERSTAND YOUR NEW DRESS CODE POLICY, MR. CATBERT.
MAYBE YOU'RE INSANE.
S. Adams E-mail: SCOTTADAMS@AOL.COM
IT'S SIMPLE. FRIDAYS ARE "CASUAL." BUT YOU CAN'T WEAR JEANS BECAUSE JEANS LOOK GOOD AND FEEL GOOD AND YOU ALREADY OWN SEVERAL PAIRS.
8/8 © 1995 United Feature Syndicate, Inc. (NYC)
IT'S ANOTHER SADISTIC HUMAN RESOURCES PLOT TO MAKE PEOPLE QUIT!!
SAY HELLO TO UNSIGHTLY PANTY LINES.

WELL, IT WOULDN'T BE FRIDAY IF I DIDN'T SEE ALICE WEARING HER ONE PAIR OF TAN PANTS.
S. Adams E-mail: SCOTTADAMS@AOL.COM
I LOVE THE "BUSINESS CASUAL" LOOK FOR THE WAY IT COMBINES UNATTRACTIVE WITH UNPROFESSIONAL WHILE DIMINISHING NEITHER.
8/9 © 1995 United Feature Syndicate, Inc. (NYC)
DO YOU THINK THE FASHION OPINION OF A MALE ENGINEER MATTERS TO ME??
TWINS!

I THOUGHT IT NECESSARY TO PROVIDE DETAILED GUIDELINES TO OUR NEW CASUAL DRESS CODE.
S. Adams E-mail: SCOTTADAMS@AOL.COM
FORBIDDEN CLOTHING INCLUDES: SHORTS, TANK TOPS, TEE SHIRTS, SHIRTS WITH SLOGANS, BLUE JEANS, SNEAKERS, AND SANDALS.
© 1994 United Feature Syndicate, Inc.
MY MORALE IS SOARING.
APPENDIX "A" IS THE APPROVED UNDERWEAR LIST.

EMPLOYEE RECOGNITION PROGRAMS

Recognition programs send an important message to all the employees in the group, not just the "winners." Specifically, the message is this: "Here's another person who won't be downsized until after we nail *you*."

But that's not the only benefit. Recognition programs help identify which social caste the employees belong to.

RECOGNITION PROGRAM	CASTE
Employee of the Month Program	"Paper Hat" Caste
Certificate of Appreciation	"No Overtime Pay" Caste
Token Cash Award	"Mushroom in the Cubicle" Caste
None	"Executive" Caste

There are no recognition programs at the highest levels of the organization. This is a motivating factor for lower-level employees. They know that if they work hard they have a chance of reaching a level of management where "recognition" programs don't exist.

I once won a "Recognition Award" at Pacific Bell. As I approached the front of the room to accept my award it became apparent that the executive running the program didn't know what I did for a living. Thinking quickly, he invented an entirely fictitious project for the benefit of the audience and thanked me for my valuable contribution to its success.

I felt "happier" after that, but my self-esteem didn't increase enough for me to think it was a good time to ask for a raise. Morale-wise, this was a home run for the company. I was so motivated that I gave serious thought to working right through my siesta that afternoon.

From E-mail: The All-Time Most Humiliating Recognition Program Ever

From: (name withheld)
To: scottadams@aol.com

Scott,

In the wake of a recent senior staff retreat, it was announced that as a reward for outstanding work, one employee would be selected each month to receive the "Fuzzy Bunny" award. Another employee, dressed in a rabbit suit (I swear I am not making this up) would visit the chosen employee's cubicle bearing balloons, a coffee mug, and a certificate of merit. This would presumably encourage us to work harder. The plan was killed (thank God) because nobody would agree to be the bunny.

UNDERVALUING EMPLOYEE CONTRIBUTIONS

Employees like to feel that their contributions are being valued. That's why managers try to avoid that sort of thing. With value comes self-esteem, and with self-esteem comes unreasonable requests for money.

There are many ways to tell employees that their work is not valued. Here are some of the crueler methods, which incidentally work the best:

- Leaf through a magazine while the employee voices an opinion.

- Ask for information "urgently" and then let it sit on your desk untouched for weeks.

- Have your secretary return calls for you.

- Use an employee's document for something other than its intended purpose, as in this example:

MAKING THEM WAIT

One of the most effective methods of humiliation used by managers is the practice of ignoring an underling who is in or near the manager's office while the manager pursues seemingly unimportant tasks. This sends a message that the employee has no human presence. It is similar to changing clothes in front of the family pet; the animal is watching but it couldn't possibly matter.

This tool of humiliation can be fine-tuned to any level simply by adjusting what activities are performed while the employee waits.

ACTIVITY	LEVEL OF HUMILIATION
Taking phone calls	Not so bad
Reading other things	Bad
Flossing	Very bad
Learning a foreign language	Very very bad

3

BUSINESS COMMUNICATION

Any business school professor will tell you that the objective of business communication is the clear transfer of information. That's why professors rarely succeed in business.

The real objective of business communication is to advance your career. That objective is generally at odds with the notion of "clear transfer of information."

The successful manager knows that the best kind of communication is one that conveys the message "I am worthy of promotion" without accidentally transferring any other information. Clear communication can only get you in trouble. Remember, you can't be wrong unless you take a position. Don't fall into that trap.

MISSION STATEMENT

If your employees are producing low-quality products that no sane person would buy, you can often fix that problem by holding meetings to discuss your Mission Statement.

A Mission Statement is defined as "a long awkward sentence that demonstrates management's inability to think clearly." All good companies have one.

Companies that don't have Mission Statements will often be under the mistaken impression that the objective of the company is to bicker among departments, produce low-quality products, and slowly go out of business. That misperception can be easily cured by writing a Mission Statement such as this:

Mission

"We will produce the highest quality products, using empowered team dynamics in a new Total Quality paradigm until we become the industry leader."

But you're not home free yet. The company Mission Statement will be meaningless until all the individual departments write their own Mission Statements to support the company's overall mission. That can be a bit harder because most departments have a variety of distinct functions and you wouldn't want to leave any of them out. So you might end up with individual Mission Statements that look like this:

Mission

"Perform world-class product development, financial analysis, and fleet services using empowered team dynamics in a Total Quality paradigm until we become the industry leader."

Individually, the Mission Statement of the company and the Mission Statement of the department might mean nothing. But taken together you can see how they would inspire employees to greater heights.

VISION

If for some reason the company's Mission Statements do not cause a turn-around in profitability, you might need a Vision Statement. In stark contrast to the detailed road map provided by a Mission Statement, a Vision Statement is more of a "high-level" guide for the company. The higher the better, because you want a vision that will last the ages.

The first step in developing a Vision Statement is to lock the managers in a room and have them debate what is meant by a "Vision Statement" and how exactly it differs from a "Mission Statement" or a "Business Plan" or "Objectives." These are important questions, because one wrong move and the employees will start doing "vision things" when they should be doing "mission things" and before long it will be impossible to sort it all out.

The debate over the definition of "vision" will end as soon as the participants become too tired and cranky to enjoy belittling each other's intelligence. At that point somebody will start suggesting various visions just to get the meeting over with. All good Vision Statements are created by groups of people with bloated bladders who would rather be doing anything else.

You know you've got a rockin' Vision Statement when it inspires the employees to think of themselves as being involved in something much more important than their pathetic little underpaid jobs, when they feel part of a much larger plan—something that can shape the society they live in. Here are examples of successful Vision Statements:

Example #1

"We will have all the wealth in the world while everybody else dies in the gutter wishing they were us."

Example #2

"We will evolve into pure energy and exist on a new temporal plane, BUWHAHAHAHAHA!!!!"

Example #3

"A computer on every desktop."*

NAMING YOUR GROUP

One of the toughest challenges in corporate communications is to develop a name for your department that makes you sound vital to the company

*This is Microsoft's actual Vision Statement.

without attracting too much work. You can do this by using empty but important-sounding words like "excellence" and "technology" and "district" in your name.

Your name should be vague enough to legitimately claim responsibility for anything that looks like it might be a success. If the CEO suddenly develops a hot interest in multimedia, you can swoop in and say, "That sounds like a job for the 'Excellence in Technology District'—because it requires technology and excellence." It's a hard argument to refute.

Then after six months, when the winds change, or you get a new CEO, and you've steered the project onto a sandbar, you can say, "Our work is done. I think this project needs to be championed by Marketing." Then transfer the responsibility, but not the budget. (Colloquially, "Throw that dead cat into somebody else's backyard.")

It may be necessary to rename your group every several months, just to avoid getting a bad reputation. Luckily there is no shortage of empty but important-sounding words to choose from. Depending on your area of expertise, you can generate new names for your group by randomly combining words from this handy list:

Technology Jobs

Information
Technology
Development
Implementation

User
Advanced
Multimedia
Data
Services
Systems
Computing
Telecommunications
Network
Research
Support

Marketing Jobs

Market
Product
Channel
Development
Communications
Evangelist
Promotions

Sales Jobs

Customer
Client
Representative
Service
Center

TALKING LIKE A MANAGER

If you want to advance in management you have to convince other people that you're smart. This is accomplished by substituting incomprehensible jargon for common words.

For example, a manager would never say, "I used my fork to eat a potato." A manager would say, "I utilized a multitined tool to process a starch resource." The two sentences mean almost the same thing, but the second one is obviously from a smarter person.

ANNOUNCEMENTS

The purpose of a company announcement is to convey the message that something is happening—something that you aren't important enough to be informed about in any meaningful detail. But if you're clever, you can sometimes read between the lines and understand the true meaning, as in this example:

MOTIVATIONAL TALKS

You may have a bunch of undertrained employees who are using inadequate tools, mired in bureaucratic processes, all of which makes your company uncompetitive. The solution is motivational talks. Gather your team together and put the "fire in their bellies" with your own brand of inspirational oratory.

It's not important that your words carry any specific useful information. As I've already explained, information can never lead to anything good. The goal is to elevate the employees to a competitive frenzy, and for that you need not transfer any information. Here are some phrases that have been known to inspire troops through the ages:

Inspirational Messages

- "It's going to be a very tough year."
- "Frankly, I don't think our project will get funded."
- "Don't expect much in terms of raises. Work should be its own reward."

- "If we don't have more profits next year we'll have more layoffs. Actually, we'll probably have more layoffs anyway."
- "There are no reorganizations planned. It's business as usual."

PRESENTATIONS

Throughout your career you will be asked to make many presentations. The purpose of a presentation is to transfer resources away from accomplishing objectives and concentrate them on explaining how well you're doing.

DILBERT, PUT TOGETHER A PRESENTATION FOR THE BIG BOSS'S STAFF MEETING.
ON WHAT TOPIC?
I HEAR THE BIG BOSS WAS A GEOMETRY MAJOR, SO LET'S WORK THAT IN SOMEHOW.
CAN YOU DO AN HOUR ON THE MANY USES OF RECTANGLES?
© 1991 United Feature Syndicate, Inc.

I'M PUTTING TOGETHER A PRESENTATION FOR THE BIG BOSS'S STAFF MEETING. WE HEAR HE LIKES GEOMETRY.
"RECTANGLES: THE MISUNDERSTOOD PARALLELOGRAMS"
IT'S BOUND TO SPARK CONTROVERSY.
WE BELIEVE IN OPEN COMMUNICATION.
© 1991 United Feature Syndicate, Inc.

THIS NEXT TRANSPARENCY IS AN INCOMPREHENSIBLE JUMBLE OF COMPLEXITY AND UNDEFINED ACRONYMS.
YOU MIGHT WONDER WHY I'M GOING TO SHOW IT TO YOU SINCE THE ONLY POSSIBLE RESULT IS TO LOWER YOUR OPINION OF MY COMMUNICATION SKILLS.
FRANKLY, IT'S BECAUSE I LIKE MAKING COMPLEX PICTURES MORE THAN I LIKE YOU.
E-mail: SCOTTADAMS@AOL.COM
© 1995 United Feature Syndicate, Inc.(NYC)

PLEASE EXCUSE THE ARTWORK IN THIS NEXT DIAGRAM.
WHAT'S THAT? IT LOOKS LIKE ELVIS' FACE ON A CREDENZA! HA HA HA! OR IS IT A RORSCHACH TEST??! HA HA HA!!
AND IN CONCLUSION, I HATE YOU ALL.
E-Mail: SCOTTADAMS@AOL.COM
© 1993 United Feature Syndicate, Inc.

GROUP WRITING

Stephen King writes very scary books. Shakespeare wrote several excellent plays. Unfortunately, they worked alone.* If only they had worked together there's no telling how much better the results would have been. That's the theory behind "group writing," and it's hard to find fault with the logic.

You've heard the saying that if you put a thousand monkeys in a room with a thousand typewriters and waited long enough, eventually you would have a room full of dead monkeys. (Tip: It's a good idea to feed monkeys.) Group writing is a lot like a room full of dead monkeys, except not as "fun."

*Some scholars contend that Shakespeare had other people write his plays and all he did was grab the credit while making crude jokes about his codpiece. Either way, you have to admire his spunk.

The main goal of group writing is to ensure that every sentence satisfies all the objectives of every person in the room. This can be problematic if all the participants have different objectives. You can minimize the impact of different objectives by focusing on the goals that all parties can agree on:

1. Don't convey any information whatsoever.

2. See number one.

The best of all worlds is to be asked to comment on the writing of a co-worker. You get to savor the experience of shredding another person's ego while taking no personal risk. It can be very satisfying.

For fun, suggest changes that would completely reverse the message intended by the author. This puts the author in the awkward position of having to reroute the document for further unhelpful comments or choosing to ignore your "upgrades." If your comments are ignored you have the God-given right to ridicule the end product and claim you had no input. Your activity will look just like "work" even though it's easy and it requires no personal risk. And on the off chance that the document you ridiculed becomes successful you can claim it as part of your accomplishments.

EXAMPLES OF CLEAR BUSINESS COMMUNICATION

From: (name withheld)
To: scottadams@aol.com

Scott,

Some years ago, I was in the habit of sending my staff a yearly recap memo, what we did, what we were looking forward to, etc. We were going to be installing an automated system and I said that even though we had accomplished a lot the past year we couldn't stand pat during the coming year.

A day after the memo was handed out, a woman asked to see me and then, after breaking down into tears, asked what did I have against a co-worker of hers, a woman whose first name was Patricia. It seems Patricia was herself very upset and crying in the ladies' room because the both of them couldn't understand for the life of them why I couldn't "stand pat."

Oh well . . .

From: (name withheld)
To: scottadams@aol.com

Scott,

My boss had these in my performance planning for 1995. (Really!)
I just got them today.
"Utilize issue clarification processes."
"Make sure appropriate people are involved in the process."
"Visibly act or function as a team player."
"Act in the best interests of achieving the team."
These are the ones I came up with. I think mine are better.
"Streamline processes for maximizing propensities."
"Enable full contrivances of empowerment."
"Eliminate occurrences of proliferate randomness."
"Managerially balance data compilation with process ownership."

From: (name withheld)
To: scottadams@aol.com

Scott,

Please help me interpret the instructions from my team leader, as
the drop-dead date is approaching.
No joke, this is real . . .
———
(1) Validate the supporting activities and remaining gaps,
(2) Identify any new gaps, and
(3) Determine the year-end stage assessment.
When determining the attainment stage, please use following cri-
teria:
(1) The attainment stage defines seven [an acronym].
Clarifications listed in the attachment called [a filename] apply.

(2) The solutions to the gaps will be developed and implemented as indicated in attachment marked [a filename].

(3) The Attainment Definition with the lowest attainment stage governs the Management Practice Attainment Stage (i.e., if a management practice has four attainment definitions with no gaps and one attainment definition with a gap, the attainment stage for the management practice is that of the attainment definition with the gap).

HELP!!!!

From: (name withheld)
To: scottadams@aol.com

Scott,

The following is an excerpt from an announcement memo from one of our general managers concerning a personnel change.

"This change will allow us to better leverage our talent base in an area where developmental roles are under way and strategically focuses us toward the upcoming Business System transition where Systems literacy and accuracy will be essential to maintain and to further improve service levels to our customer base going forward."

Several of us sat down and tried to understand what was supposed to be communicated and came up with the following by just crossing out most of the double-talk:

"This change will improve service to our customers."

From: (name withheld)
To: scottadams@aol.com

Scott,

The dean here in the college of business (call him upper manage-ment) wanted the faculty to develop a "Mission Statement" that we would all be willing to "own." But he knew he couldn't get 110 peo-ple to work together on anything, let alone a Mission Statement. So he formed a committee.

Guess what the committee did. Right—it split into groups and drafted all 110 faculty to be part of those various groups. We formed "teams" which were supposed to "determine our core competency" and find a way to "satisfy our customers" in the context of "continu-ous improvement" (preferably on half of the current budget).

The result was predictable. Some of us resented the waste of our time, some of us used witty, yet biting sarcasm, and some actually thought it was a great opportunity to "get to know each other better." These guys were the ones who asked us all to hold hands at com-mencement because "You are special. This is a very special moment."

The final product was a document no one would support. We all got a note from the dean that essentially said, "You didn't read my mind and got the wrong answer!"

4

GREAT LIES OF MANAGEMENT

For your convenience I have compiled and numbered the most popular management lies of all time. I do this as a service to the business community. Now when you're telling a story about the treachery of your managers you can simply refer to each lie by its number, for example, "She told us number six and we all went back to our cubicles and laughed." This will save you a lot of energy that can then be channeled into whining about your co-workers.

Great Lies of Management

1. "Employees are our most valuable asset."

2. "I have an open-door policy."

3. "You could earn more money under the new plan."

4. "We're reorganizing to better serve our customers."

5. "The future is bright."

6. "We reward risk-takers."

7. "Performance will be rewarded."

8. "We don't shoot the messenger."

9. "Training is a high priority."

10. "I haven't heard any rumors."

11. "We'll review your performance in six months."

12. "Our people are the best."

13. "Your input is important to us."

It's not always easy to tell the difference between a scurrilous management lie and ordinary nitwittism. When confronted with an ambiguous situation you can usually sniff out the truth by using a handy method that I call the "What Is More Likely" test. Here's how it works:

State each of the plausible interpretations of reality (using humorous metaphors when possible), then ask yourself this question:

"What is more likely?"

You will discover that this technique will greatly clarify the communications of your managers. Allow me to demonstrate its usefulness on the Great Lies of Management.

"EMPLOYEES ARE OUR MOST VALUABLE ASSET"

On the surface this statement seems to be at odds with the fact that companies are treating their "most valuable assets" the same way a leaf blower treats leaves. How can this apparent contradiction be explained?

An example will be useful. Let's say your boss has a broken desk chair and there's no money left in the budget to replace it. Is it more likely that your boss would:

A. Sit on the floor until the next budget cycle.

B. Use a nonmanagement chair despite the lower status it confers on the sitter.

C. Postpone filling a job opening in the group, distribute the extra work to the "most valuable assets," and use the savings to buy a proper chair.

As employees we like to think we're more valuable than the office furniture. But the "What Is More Likely" test indicates that it's not the case. Realistically we're someplace toward the lower end of the office supply hierarchy.

I used to take great pride in opening a new box of staples and informing them that they worked for me and I was their undisputed ruler. But eventually I had to stop naming them individually because it was such an emotional roller coaster when one went crooked. This may be off the point but if anybody sees Walter, tell him I miss him.

"I HAVE AN OPEN-DOOR POLICY"

What is more likely?

A. Your boss genuinely wants a never-ending trail of Bozos to walk into her office and complain about things that can't be fixed. Her long-term goal is to be distracted from her real responsibilities, fail in her job, and eventually become homeless.

Or . . .

B. She knows she can intimidate people into avoiding her office by scowling and assigning work to the first ten people who try it. That way she gets the benefit of sounding "open" without any of the costs.

"YOU COULD EARN MORE MONEY UNDER THE NEW PLAN"

Is it likely that your company changed the entire compensation plan to give all of you more money? Are raises so rare these days that your company actually forgot about that option?

Or is it more likely that the new compensation system is a complicated maneuver to disguise the fact that from now on your health benefits will be administered by the Christian Scientists?

"WE'RE REORGANIZING TO BETTER SERVE OUR CUSTOMERS"

Is it likely that the current reorganization—in stark contrast to all the ones that preceded it—will be the one that turns your company into a revenue-generating dynamo? And is it likely that the main reason your customers hate you is that your organization chart is suboptimal?

Or is it more likely that your management has no clue how to fix your fundamental problems and they think that rearranging the existing supply of nitwits will look like progress?

22 BUILD A BETTER LIFE BY STEALING OFFICE SUPPLIES Dogbert's Big Book of Business

"THE FUTURE IS BRIGHT"

Is it likely that your boss is a visionary who can predict the future even though he can't operate the computer on his desk? And if he can see the future, is it likely that he prefers to waste this ability in his current job versus using his powers to cure cancer and make a few bucks in the process?

Or is it more likely that the future isn't much brighter than your boss?

"WE REWARD RISK-TAKERS"

By definition, risk-takers often fail. So do morons. In practice it's difficult to sort them out.

Is it likely that your manager will begin rewarding people who have failed, knowing that a good portion of them are morons and every one of them has caused the boss to receive at least one executive-induced wedgie?

Or is it more likely that people who fail will be assigned to Quality Teams while the people who succeed will leave the company faster than a cheetah leaves a salad bar?

Bonus Question

If the successful people leave, will they make more money or less money at another company?

"PERFORMANCE WILL BE REWARDED"

Is it likely that this is the year the officers of your company will say, "To hell with the stock prices and our bonuses. What were we thinking? Let's distribute more money to the employees!"?

Or is it more likely you'll be put through a tortuous Performance Review process that would result in approximately the same tiny raise whether you were Mother Teresa or the Unabomber?

"WE DON'T SHOOT THE MESSENGER"

Is it likely that all the managers of your company have simultaneously found Buddha dancing in their desk drawers and decided to give peace a chance?

Or is it more likely that these Satan-spawned, coffee-torqued managers will continue to extract revenge on any target that is dumb enough to stand still?

(Note: It helps to add a little "attitude" to some of these questions to increase the contrast.)

"TRAINING IS A HIGH PRIORITY"

Let's say, hypothetically, that the budget for your department gets tight. Is it more likely your manager will leave your high-priority training budget intact and save money by delaying the launch of your product instead, thus reducing his own raise and bonus?

Or is it more likely that the training budget will disappear faster than the hors d'oeuvres at a Richard Simmons *Sweatin' to the Oldies* reunion.

From E-mail . . .

From: (name withheld)
To: scottadams@aol.com

Scott,

. . . an experience I had with [company] a few years ago. A survey determined that employees required more training. At the same time, training budgets were slashed drastically. I was literally forced to attend a bunch of little $39 Holiday Inn training sessions on time management, etc.

"I HAVEN'T HEARD ANY RUMORS"

Is it likely that the perpetual flow of rumors has suddenly stopped just at the time when the odds are highest that something might actually happen?

Or is it more likely that your manager knows the news is so bad that the slightest whiff of the truth will make the employees less productive than a truckload of Chihuahuas?*

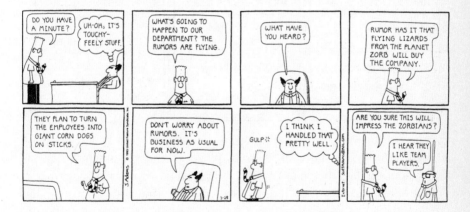

*Maybe this analogy is a stretch. But just maybe I've done exhaustive studies of Chihuahua work habits and discovered that a truckload of Chihuahuas is the least productive organizational size.

"WE'LL REVIEW YOUR PERFORMANCE IN SIX MONTHS"

The best thing about the future is that it isn't here yet. When your manager promises to review your performance in six months for a possible raise, what is more likely?

A. Your manager believes that you could become smarter and more productive in 180 days, thus earning such a large increase in salary that you'll be glad you waited.

Or . . .

B. Your manager expects he will be in a new job within six months and your chances of getting a raise are deader than a Fishstick at a cat festival.

"OUR PEOPLE ARE THE BEST"

This lie is appreciated by the employees. Unfortunately only one company in each industry can have the best employees. And you might be suspicious about the fact that your company pays the lowest salaries.

Is it likely that the "best" employees would be drawn to your company despite the lower-than-average pay? Is it possible that there's a strange mental condition that makes some people brilliant at their jobs, yet unable to compare two salary numbers and determine which one is higher? Let's call these people "Occupational Savants." If they exist, what are the odds that they all decided to work at your company?

And is it likely that the people you work with all day appear to be denser than titanium, yet in reality are the most skilled professionals in their field?

Or is it more likely that the Nobel Prize–winning economists of the world are right—the market system works—and your company has exactly the doltish quality of employees that it's willing to pay for?

"YOUR INPUT IS IMPORTANT TO US"

To the manager, the following equation holds true:

$$\text{Employee Input} = \text{More Work} = \text{Bad}$$

As an abused and powerless employee you know it's fun to give your manager impractical suggestions such as this:

"If you care about the health of the employees you should ask the CEO to fund research on the effects of fluorescent lights on fertility."

This suggestion is thoroughly impractical, but the beauty of it is that your manager can't discard it offhand without appearing uncaring. Nor can the work be delegated, since no manager wants a subordinate to talk to his superior and maybe say embarrassing things.

Most employee suggestions are either clueless or sadistic. Once in a great while a good idea slips through, but a good idea is indistinguishable from a bad one unless you're the person who thought of it. It's never entirely clear in advance when employee input will be a good thing. So managers have to treat all input as bad.

Here's the test to see if managers really want employee input:

Is it likely that your boss enjoys the extra work involved in pursuing the well-meaning, sagelike suggestions of your gifted colleagues?

Or is it more likely your boss will pretend to listen to your thoroughly impractical suggestions, thank you for the input, do exactly what he planned all along, and then ask you to chair the United Way campaign as punishment?

See how easy this is?

5

MACHIAVELLIAN METHODS

(WRITTEN BY DOGBERT)

This chapter contains many surefire tips for gaining wealth and personal power at the expense of people who are studying how to be team players. Naturally I have withheld my most effective tips so that I can crush you later if it's absolutely necessary, or if it just looks like fun. But what you find here should still be enough to brush aside the kindhearted dolts that litter your path to success.

Use these techniques sparingly, at least until you've gained total power over the simpletons around you. If you use all these techniques at once you'll probably scare the neighboring cubicle dwellers into thinking you're a witch. They might form an unruly mob, storm your office, and kill your secretary. This would be a tragedy, especially if you need some copies made.

PROVIDE BAD ADVICE

During the course of your career many people will come to you for advice. This is your chance to steer them off the corporate speedway and—if you're skillful—help them plow into a crowd of innocent spectators.

It's not always easy to give advice. For one thing, your tail might wag uncontrollably, thus signaling your impending treachery. Moreover, your advice has to sound plausible, no matter how destructive and self-serving it really is. The best way to give bad advice that still sounds well-meaning is to "take the high road."

For example, let's say your manager has engaged in unethical conduct and your co-worker discovers this activity and comes to you for advice. You should "take the high road." Tell your co-worker to confront the boss and also blow the whistle to the authorities. This will simultaneously open your boss's job for you while most likely eliminating your co-worker from competition, all in the name of what is "right."

You don't need to take the high road in all cases. Your co-workers might be sufficiently moronic to accept plain old bad advice without questioning it, as in these examples:

SHADE THE TRUTH

The great thing about the truth is that there are so many ways to avoid it without being a "liar." You can avoid the stigma of being a liar while still enjoying all the benefits of misleading people by simply omitting important qualifiers to your statements.

TRUE STATEMENT	OMITTED QUALIFIER
"I'm a team player"	. . . for the other team.
"You're next on my list"	. . . of things to ignore.
"I'll call you when I know"	. . . that you won't be there.
"I love what you've done with your hair"	. . . Medusa.

WHOM YOU ASSOCIATE WITH

People will judge you by the company you keep, especially during lunch.
Never eat lunch with a person of lower salary.

Exceptions

- Your secretary during National Secretaries Week (obligatory).

- Your boss's secretary (indirect sucking up).

- A person widely known to be terminally ill (makes you look compassionate).

If you get tricked into dining with a person of lower salary you can salvage the situation by spreading a rumor that the person is terminally ill. This is not technically lying, since we're all going to die eventually. If anybody spots you together, hold your napkin over your mouth like a surgical mask whenever the low-ranking person speaks to you.

Ideally, you want to dupe higher salaried people into being seen at a meal with you. They will try every trick to avoid you, so you must be nimble and devious. For example, you could schedule a department lunch and not bother to invite the other people in the department. Or, if you possess vital information that is needed by the higher-paid person, take the knowledge hostage and demand lunch as your ransom.

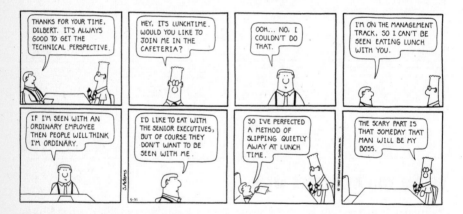

WITHHOLD INFORMATION

A good way for ineffective people to cling to power in an organization is by creating a monopoly on information. This information should seem important, but not critically important. In other words, your co-workers should want the information you're withholding, but not so badly that they'll choke you to death when you prevent them from getting it.

Form a multilayered protective defense for your strategically withheld information. With the right mixture of attitude and complete psychopathic behavior you can withhold just about anything. Here's how.

Layer One

Insist that you don't have the information and act like the requesters are insane for expecting that you do. Repeat their request aloud as if to underscore the fact that what they're asking for makes no sense. Grill them mercilessly as to why on God's green earth they would ever think you had this information. If they present a convincing case that they know you have the information, smile and act like the problem was in the way they asked the question. Go to layer two.

Layer Two

Say you're too busy to explain all the information to the requesters. Remind them that it took you years to understand it all. Ask them to leave you an easily ignored voice mail to schedule a time when you can sort through it together. That's because you "want to help." If the requesters persist, proceed to layer three.

Layer Three

Insist that the information is not ready yet—either because you're waiting for somebody else's input or because you need to "massage" the numbers to remove all the misleading data. If the requesters insist on settling for last month's information—or even misleading information—proceed to layer four.

Layer Four

Exhibit an exceptionally bad personality. Be rude, negative, and condescending. This layer is not a defense in itself, but it makes the requesters more vulnerable to the next layers of defense.

Layer Five

Give the requesters incomplete or irrelevant information and hope they go away thinking they got what they needed. By the time they get back to their offices and discover they've been duped they might be discouraged. If you did a convincing job with the layer four bad-personality step, there's a good chance the requesters will give up on you altogether and leave you safe and happy.

Damage Control

If the requesters leave your cubicle with any sort of information whatsoever, complain to anybody who will listen that the information is faulty because the requesters either didn't understand the information or misinterpreted it.

TWO WRONGS MAKE A RIGHT, ALMOST

Your simpleminded relatives were technically correct when they told you "Two wrongs don't make a right." What they failed to mention is that two wrongs can sometimes cancel each other out, and although it's not as good as a "right" it's much better than one wrong. If you're clever, you can neutralize any blunder through a series of offsetting destructive acts, as in this example:

RETRIBUTION

Retribution is your best friend, especially when it's combined with its natural companion: hypocrisy. For some reason, retribution has become a dirty little word in business. But only the word itself is a problem; the practice of retribution is as popular as ever. Use it whenever you get the chance.

While an actual act of retribution can be fun and deeply fulfilling, it's the *threat* of retribution that has the most potential to help your career. For the threat to be taken seriously you must have actual or potential power to carry out your retribution. If you're at a low level in the organization you must create the impression that you're likely to be promoted or you're likely to be having an affair with somebody in power. If you're ugly and unlikely to be "bopping up" then your best bet is to create an aura of imminent promotion by simply looking managerial:

- Dress more expensively than your peers.

- Conceal any traces of technical competence.

- Use the word "paradigm" several times a day.

- Tell everybody that you're preparing for a meeting with the president.

- Refer to articles from the *Wall Street Journal.*°

These things are not enough to guarantee a promotion—although they come close—but they're enough to make your peers hedge their bets and do some preemptive butt kissing.

All your threats of retribution will seem hollow unless you can demonstrate your ability to detect those transgressions that merit retribution even when they occur beyond your presence. One way to appear all-knowing is to build a reliable network of spies in the organization.

°Don't waste your time actually reading the *Wall Street Journal*. Many people subscribe to it, but nobody actually reads it. It's easier just to say, "Hey, did you see that article in the *Journal* yesterday?" and see what happens. If the other person says yes, he's bluffing too, so you can both give a hearty laugh about the insights of the article and leave it at that. If the other person indicates he did not read the article, give a condescending look and mutter, "It figures" before changing the subject.

The best way to encourage spies to give *you* information is by being willing to give *them* information in exchange—preferably false information. Don't be afraid to invent plausible-sounding rumors that you know won't pan out. Inaccurate rumors are often an indication that you have direct contacts in the inner circles of the organization where lots of ideas are floated that don't materialize. Always couch your rumors in weasel terms like "They're considering . . ." or "One of the plans is . . ." so you can't be proven wrong no matter what happens.

The final and most important part of making retribution work for you is to broadcast your intention to use it, as in this example:

VIRUS MANEUVER

If you're in charge of a project that's a sure loser, or if the people who work for you are losers, you must distance yourself from them as soon as possible. The direct method is to simply switch jobs or fire your bad employees. But that's settling for too little. Instead, think of your bad assets as potential viruses that can be used to infect your enemies within the corporation. All you need to do is artificially inflate their value and wait for some unsuspecting manager to try to take them off your hands.

Never make the mistake of giving bad Performance Reviews to bad employees. That will limit their ability to switch jobs within the company and shackle them to you forever until their corrosive effect destroys you. It's better to focus on the positive aspects of every employee's performance, even if you have to assault the truth a bit.

If you can't transfer bad employees to other departments, move them into positions in which they are the key support for projects that are closely identified with other managers. If that opportunity doesn't exist, as a last resort, put the poor performers in charge of the United Way campaign and let everybody suffer with you.

DEMAGOGUERY

You can achieve notoriety by speaking out against things that are already unpopular. The focus of your attacks could be a project, technology, or strategy, or even an incompetent manager. There will be no shortage of worthy targets to choose from. But pick carefully. Make sure your target is already doomed and despised. When the inevitable happens, you'll look like a genius for accurately forecasting collapse.

Here are some good examples of projects for which you can confidently predict failure:

- Any morale building effort.

- Any large-scale reengineering effort.

- Any project that takes more than two years.

- Any market-driven technology product.

- Anything that hasn't been done before.

By sheer chance, some of the projects that you attack will succeed. But no project is so thoroughly successful that you can't pick out a few weak areas and highlight them as examples of "just what you were afraid would happen."

Once you've built a track record for consistently forecasting the failure of other people's work, higher-level managers will begin to think you're a brilliant visionary. Promotion is inevitable, at which point you'll be in a much better position to take advantage of other people for personal gain.

DISPARAGE CO-WORKERS

All success is relative. You can improve your relative success by disparaging the skills and accomplishments of those who surround you. This will be fairly easy since the people who surround you are idiots. Focus like a laser on every misstep they make and take every opportunity to broadcast the mistakes to your boss in clever ways that don't make you look like a backstabber.

You can avoid the backstabber appearance by badmouthing your peers to your boss's secretary. This guarantees that the information will reach your boss without your direct involvement, and as a bonus the facts usually become exaggerated in the process. Best of all, once the boss's secretary believes your co-workers are losers, they won't be able to schedule time on the boss's calendar to prove otherwise.

Don't make the mistake of criticizing your co-workers to their faces. That will tip your hand and invite retaliation. The only constructive criticism is the kind you do behind people's backs.

FORM OVER SUBSTANCE

The earth is populated by shallow and ignorant people. That's why form will always be more important than substance. You can waste your time complaining about how that should not be the case in a perfect world, or you can snap out of it and follow my advice.

Documents

If a document is over two pages long, few people will ever read it. And those who do read it won't remember it in twenty-four hours. That's why all your documents should be over two pages long. You don't want your readers to be influenced by a bunch of facts. You want them to look at your creative use of fonts, your brilliant application of white space, and your inspired graphics. Good formatting leaves the reader with the clear impression that you are a genius and therefore whatever you're writing about must be a good idea.

Clothing

Contrary to popular belief, it's often your clothing that gets promoted, not you. You reap some benefit by being the person inside the clothes. Always dress better than your peers so your clothes will be the ones selected for promotion. And make sure you're in your clothes when it happens. One man made the mistake of bringing his dry cleaning to work and ended up as a direct report to his own sports jacket.

Looking Busy

Never walk down the hall without a document in your hands. People with documents in their hands look like hardworking employees heading for important meetings. People with nothing in their hands look like they're heading for the cafeteria. People with the newspaper in their hands look like they're heading for the bathroom.

Above all, make sure you carry loads of stuff home with you at night, thus generating the false impression that you work longer hours than you do.

APPEAL TO GREED

You can short-circuit the two or three neurons that people use for common sense by appealing to their greed. Nothing defines humans better than their willingness to do irrational things in the pursuit of phenomenally unlikely payoffs. This is the principle behind lotteries, dating, and religion. You can use this quirk of human nature to your advantage and it won't cost you a dime.

The psychological explanation for this phenomenon is that life sucks and we'd all rather fantasize about being someplace else. Your job as a Machiavellian manipulator is to give people a microscopic chance of gaining riches by doing your bidding.

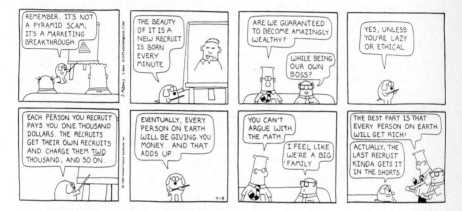

GET OTHERS TO DO YOUR WORK

Take every opportunity to delegate the unglamorous and hopeless portions of your workload downward, sideways, and upward.

Delegating to subordinates is easy. The hard part is delegating to co-workers and your boss. Always appeal to the principle of "efficiency" when you try to fob off your work sideways or upward. Support your argument by creating a record of being incompetent and unreliable for any tasks that are boring or thankless.

For example, if you are put in charge of bringing the donuts to the staff meeting, bring the kind that nobody likes. If you are asked to type up notes from the meeting, intentionally write bad grammar into people's quotes. If you are asked to chair the company's United Way campaign, start each meeting by stating your opinion that these people should "get a job and stop freeloading." Eventually, you'll be in a much stronger position to convincingly say things like "Well, I could make those photocopies, but in the interest of efficiency, Ted would do a much better job."

But the real "low-hanging fruit" of work avoidance involves any task that has more importance to somebody else than it has to you. If you ignore this type of task long enough, eventually the person who really needs it done will offer to do it, even if it's clearly your job.

EXAGGERATE YOUR TALENTS

Everybody exaggerates his or her talents. There's no trick to that. You need to take it to the next level: complete fantasy. It's not enough to say you performed well at your assigned tasks; you must take credit for any positive development that ever happened in the company or on earth.

What You Did	What You Can Claim
Attended some meetings, ate donuts, nodded head to bluff comprehension.	Created a strategy to bring the company into the next century. Increased revenues by $25 million.
Worked on a project that got canceled after management figured out what you were doing.	Reengineered the company's core processes and increased market share by ninety percent.

Got stuck organizing the company's U.S. Savings Bond drive.

Stabilized the monetary system of the wealthiest nation on earth.

INTIMIDATION BY LOUDNESS

Speak loudly and act irrationally. Co-workers and even bosses will bend to your will if you use this method consistently. Consistency is the key. Send a clear signal that you cannot be swayed by reason and that you'll never stop being loud and obnoxious until you get your way. This method is effective because the law prevents people from killing you and there's no other practical way to make you stop.

At first, your victim might try to wait you out, hoping you'll get tired and go away. That's where most Machiavellian wannabes fail with the loudness method—they give up too early. You must be persistent, bordering on loony. Never let up.

After you get your way, turn instantly into the sweetest person your victim has ever seen. Buy candy. Call the victim's boss and leave kudos. Sing the victim's praise while others are nearby. This widens the gap between the experience people have when they satisfy you and the experience they have when they don't.

This method is most effective when used on people who were raised in dysfunctional families. Fortunately, that's nearly everybody. These people will start to believe you're their best personal friend. At that point you can abuse them even more.

MANAGE SEXY PROJECTS

The worth of any project is based on how it will sound on your résumé. Don't get caught up in the propaganda about how important something is for the stockholders. The stockholders are people you'll never meet. And since most projects fail or turn into something you never intended, the only lasting impact of your work is the impact on your résumé. Keep your priorities straight.

Nobody can read a résumé and get any real sense of what the author actually did on a job. All judgments are necessarily based on the collective quality of the individual words. That's why you have to work on projects that have good words in the names.

Avoid any project that has one of the following words in its description:

- Accounting

- Operations

- Reduction

- Budget

- Quality

- Analysis

Seek out any project that has one of the following résumé-ready words in its description:

- Multimedia

- Worldwide

- Advanced

- Strategic

- Revenue

- Market

- Technology

- Rapid

- Competitive

GET INPUT (BUY-IN)

Many dolts will try to impede your brilliant plans. You can minimize their collective resistance through a process called "getting buy-in." This involves collecting the opinions of people who care about a decision, acting interested, then pretending that your plan is a direct reflection of what the majority of people want.

This might sound silly, but if you compare it to the alternatives it's the only practical solution. You can't accommodate a hundred different opinions, and you can't ignore them. All you can do is provide people with the illusion that they participated in the decision. For some reason, that's enough to make people happy.° This is the basis for all democracies.

SELF-SERVING STRATEGIES

There are documented cases of employees who experienced low-level food poisoning in the company cafeteria and later, when this was combined with the hypnotic trance state induced by the boredom of the job, reacted to the inspirational message on a company bulletin board and accidentally acted in the best interest of the company.

It could happen to you. Just be careful what you eat. That's the best advice I can give.

MANIPULATE THE MEDIA

Reporters are faced with the daily choice of painstakingly researching stories or writing whatever people tell them. Both approaches pay the same.

Contrary to what you might believe, the quotes that you see in news stories are rarely what was actually said and rarely in the original context. Most quotes are engineered by the writers to support whatever notion they had before starting the story. Avoid any mention of a name or topic that you wouldn't want to see yourself misquoted about.

°The reason would be that people are idiots.

For example, see how an innocuous corporate statement can be edited slightly to alter the original meaning while still being a legitimate quote:

You say: "Our company is skilled in many other things that are never reported by the biased media."

Media reports: "Our company _____killed _____m_____other t_____er_____e____s_____a.”

All news stories focus on one of two things: something that is very bad or something that is very good. Help the writer determine what is very good about your situation; otherwise the default story is generally about something that is very bad.

THE HONESTY TRAP

You might be tempted to give your honest opinions to upper-level managers. Resist this temptation at all costs.

Don't be lulled into a sense of false security by management's oft-stated interest in getting feedback. There are only two safe things to say to a manager:

- "Your decisions are brilliant!"
- "I have an idea on how to save some paper!"

Any other feedback is a direct challenge to the manager's intelligence and authority. If your impulse for honesty grows too strong, try this simple exercise to tame your masochistic tendencies:

1. Find a large kitchen spatula.

2. Beat yourself on the head with it.

3. Repeat.

TAKE CREDIT FOR THE WORK OF OTHERS

Millions of employees do millions of things every day. By sheer chance, some of them will accidentally do something valuable. Identify these rare situations and make every effort to attach your name to them.

If you're the boss, make sure your name is prominently written on any piece of good work produced by your people. Your people will hate that, but if you've studied the section on retribution it won't be a problem.

If you're part of a team effort, make sure you're the one who presents the conclusions and distributes the documents to upper management. Staple your business card to documents when you distribute them. That makes you look like the primary contributor even if all you did during the meetings was eat donuts and fantasize about making love to an attractive co-worker in the utility closet.

OFFER FALSE SACRIFICES

An essential part of being a team player is the willingness to make false sacrifices that other people perceive as genuine. Offer to give up things that you know won't be accepted or won't be missed. Here are some good things to offer up as sacrifices:

- Offer to reduce the rate of increase in future budgets and refer to it frequently as a budget reduction.

- Transfer your worst employees to another department to "help."

- Reduce your budget by shutting down a project that was doomed to fail because of your management.

- Offer to fire employees in your department who were supporting other groups in the company. The managers of the other groups will have to do the fighting to rebuild your empire while you look like a team player for offering the sacrifice.

- Offer to cut support to the most critical function in the company. This offer will never be accepted and it makes the things you didn't offer seem like they must be comparatively more important.

WORK ON PROJECTS WITH NO VERIFIABLE RESULTS

The best jobs are those that have results that cannot be measured. Stay away from jobs in which your value can be measured in quantity and time-liness. You can exaggerate your impact on quality much more easily than you can exaggerate your impact on quantity.

Bad Jobs

> Sales
> Programming
> Operations

Customer service
Shipping

Great Jobs

Strategy
Anything with "Media" in the name
Marketing (for mature products)
Long-term reengineering projects
Advertising
Procurement

SEND PEOPLE TO THE LEGAL DEPARTMENT

From time to time it will be necessary for you to kill a project without being identified as the assassin. That's why large companies have legal departments. No project is so risk-free that your company lawyer can't kill it.

MANAGE THE BUDGET GROUP

It can be unglamorous work to manage the budget function for your group. Most managers wouldn't want that duty, so it will be easy for you to move the budget tasks under your control. Once you have it, you effectively control the strategy and careers of every person in the department.

There is a widespread misconception that the budget is set by senior management and the budget analysts are merely tools of their policies. In reality of course, it's the other way around. Senior managers are so bored by the budget process, and so overwhelmed by its complexity, that they jump at the chance to accept a budget analyst's recommendation for budget changes.

SUSAN, I WANT YOU TO MAKE SOME BUDGET CUTS THROUGHOUT MY DEPARTMENT.
BUT I'M ONLY THE BUDGET ANALYST.
E-Mail: SCOTTADAMS@AOL.COM
S.Adams
3-8
I COULDN'T POSSIBLY UNDERSTAND ALL THE ENGINEERING PROJECTS ENOUGH TO MAKE INTELLIGENT CHOICES.
© 1994 United Feature Syndicate, Inc.
REALLY? GREAT! I THOUGHT IT WAS JUST ME!
SHALL I WHOMP UP A STRATEGY WHILE I'M AT IT?

6

EMPLOYEE STRATEGIES

You're working more hours than ever. And if you're one of the so-called exempt employees you aren't getting paid for overtime. It might seem that your average hourly pay is shrinking like a cheap cotton shirt.

Not true!

Nature has a way of balancing these things out. You have to consider the total compensation picture, which I call "Virtual Hourly Compensation."

Definition

Virtual Hourly Compensation is the total amount of compensation you receive per hour, including:

- Salary

- Bonuses

- Health plan

- Inflated travel reimbursement claims

- Stolen office supplies

- Airline frequent flyer awards

- Coffee

- Donuts

- Newspapers and magazines

- Personal phone calls

- Office sex

- Telecommuting

- Illegitimate sick days

- Internet surfing

- Personal e-mail

- Use of laser printer for your résumé

- Free photocopies

- Training for your next job

- Cubicle used as a retail outlet

ADAMS'S LAW OF COMPENSATION EQUILIBRIUM

Adams's Law of Compensation Equilibrium states that an employee's Virtual Hourly Compensation stays constant over time. Whenever an employer finds a way to increase your workload, nature will adjust either your compensation or your perceived work hours to create equilibrium.

For example, when companies went hog-wild on downsizing in the early nineties, the surviving employees began working longer hours to avoid identification as low performers. Salaries didn't increase much because the supply of employees was greater than the demand. On the surface, it looked as if average hourly wages were permanently lowered.

Predictably, nature responded to the temporary imbalance by creating new activities that looked like work but weren't; for example, Internet access and telecommuting.

This is the same process of deception and disguise that nature provides to other parts of the animal kingdom. For example, the Elbonian Puffer Bird can expand to twice its normal size when threatened.* Similarly, employees puff up their *perceived* hours of work without increasing their *real* work. Equilibrium is maintained.

TOTAL WORK EQUATION

Real Work + Appearance of Work = Total Work

You can be a participant in nature's grand plan by actively pursuing the activities that create equilibrium. Try to keep your *Total Work* at a constant level without increasing your *Real Work*. Do that by beefing up your *Appearance of Work* using any of the following activities:

---

*Yes, I did make that up. But we both know that somewhere there must be a bird that puffs up when it's threatened. If I'm not mistaken, my parakeet Goldie did that just before the tragic basketball incident that I later blamed on my brother.

- Internet surfing

- Personal e-mail

- Attending meetings

- Talking to your boss

- Conventions

- Upgrading your computer

- Testing new software

- Waiting for answers from co-workers

- Project consulting

- Hiding behind voice mail

TELECOMMUTING

Telecommuting is nature's gift to our generation. Just when it seemed that the combination of long commutes, pollution, congested highways, and long meetings would kill us, nature gave us telecommuting.

Now you can spend time at home, sitting around in your pajamas, listening to your stereo, and playing with your hand puppet. If you feel generous and slam out two hours of productivity, it's more than you would have done in the office, so you can feel good about it.

The office is designed for "work," not productivity. Work can be defined as "anything you'd rather not be doing." Productivity is a different matter. Telecommuting substitutes two hours of productivity for ten hours of work.

To cover your joy of telecommuting (and avoid having the program canceled because of excess joy) take every opportunity to lie about how much more "work" you do at home. Leave lots of inane and unnecessary voice mail messages to your boss and co-workers while you're home. This creates the illusion that you are as unhappy and unproductive as they are, thus justifying a continuation of telecommuting.

RUNNING A SIDE BUSINESS FROM YOUR CUBICLE

A cubicle is an excellent retail space, suitable for selling stuffed dolls, earrings, cosmetics, semiprecious gems, plant arrangements, household cleaning products, real estate, and vacation packages. Don't miss your opportunity to "moonlight," or as I like to call it, "fluorescentlight."

All you need is a tacky handmade sign on the outside of your cubicle that tells people you're open for business. A brochure or product sample can help lure people in.

You don't need high-quality merchandise. Let's be honest—if your co-workers were bright enough to know the difference between diamonds and monkey crap they wouldn't be working at your company. So don't waste a bunch of time on "quality." It's shelf space that matters, and you've got 180 cubic feet to play with. It's your chance to make some money while you're at work.

THEFT OF OFFICE SUPPLIES

Office supplies are an important part of your total compensation package. If God didn't want people to steal office supplies he wouldn't have given us briefcases, purses, and pockets. In fact, no major religion specifically bans the pilfering of office supplies.*

The only downside is the risk of being caught, disgraced, and imprisoned. But if you compare that to your current work situation I think you'll agree that it's not such a big deal.

The secret is to avoid getting too greedy. Office supplies are like compound interest—a little bit per day adds up over time. If you want some yellow sticky notes, don't take the whole box at once. Instead, use several sheets per day as page markers on documents that you're taking home. Later, carefully remove them and reassemble them into pads.

You can steal an unlimited amount of pens and pencils, but avoid the rookie mistake of continually asking the department secretary for the key to the supply closet. That attracts suspicion. Instead, steal supplies directly from your co-workers. Casually "borrow" their writing tools during meetings and never return them. Act naturally, and remember you can always laugh and claim it was a "reflex" if you get caught putting their stuff in your pocket.

---

*Some religious scholars will debate my interpretation. But ultimately it's a matter of faith.

Your co-workers will be trying to swipe your writing implements too. Defend your pens and pencils by conspicuously chewing on them during meetings. I've found that a few teeth marks are more effective than The Club in preventing theft.

If you have a home computer, say good-bye to purchasing your own diskettes. Stolen diskettes look exactly like work-related diskettes that are being taken home so you can "do a little work at night." The only practical limit on the number of diskettes you can steal is the net worth of the company you're stealing from. Your company will go broke if you steal too many diskettes. Nobody wins when that happens. That's why moderation is the key. After you have enough diskettes to back up your hard drive, and maybe shingle your house, think about cutting back.

USE COMPUTERS TO LOOK BUSY

Any time you use a computer it looks like "work" to the casual observer. You can send and receive personal e-mail, download pornography from the Internet, calculate your finances, and generally have a blast without doing anything remotely related to work. These aren't exactly the societal benefits that everybody expected from the computer revolution, but they're not bad either.

When you get caught by your boss—and you will get caught—your best defense is to claim you're teaching yourself to use the new software, thus saving valuable training dollars. You're not a loafer, you're a self-starter. Offer to show your boss what you learned. That will make your boss scurry away like a frightened salamander.*

---

*In laboratory tests, three out of four frightened salamanders were mistaken for supervisors.

WAITING FOR INFORMATION FROM CO-WORKERS

Hardly any task can be done without first getting help from other people in the company. Luckily you'll never get that help because the other people are busy trying to get help from other people too.

This situation is good news for everybody. Nobody does any real work and you can all blame your woes on some worthless bastard in another department. Simply make phone calls and wait for help that never comes. At the weekly status meeting you can legitimately claim that you've done everything you can do for now.

Boss: "Did you finish your product designs?"

You: "I made phone calls but nobody called me back."

Boss: "That's no excuse."

You: "What do you suggest?"

Boss: "Get me involved earlier if you're not getting support."

You: "I tried but you didn't call me back."

Boss: "I'm involved now. After the meeting, tell me who's not giving you proper support and I'll take care of it."

You: "I'll call you."

VOICE MAIL

Voice mail has freed more employees from work than any other innovation. Prior to voice mail, people answered the phone personally and often found themselves doing more work because of it. Now you can just let it ring until the call rolls over to voice mail. This has a triple advantage: You can (1) escape immediate work, (2) screen messages to avoid future work, and (3) create the impression that you're overworked!

Sample Voice Mail Message

"This is Scott Adams. I can't take your call because I am a martyr doing the job of several people. Although I am dying from exhaustion I'm sure that the reason you called is highly important and worthy of my attention. Please leave a detailed message so I can evaluate your importance in relation to the six hundred other messages I will get today."

7

PERFORMANCE REVIEWS

THE PURPOSE OF THE PERFORMANCE REVIEW

One of the most frightening and degrading experiences in every employee's life is the annual Performance Review.

In theory, the Performance Review process can be thought of as a positive interaction between a "coach" and an employee, working together to achieve maximum performance. In reality, it's more like finding a dead squirrel in your backyard and realizing the best solution is to fling it onto your neighbor's roof. Then your obnoxious neighbor takes it off the roof and flings it back, as if he had the right to do that. Ultimately, nobody's happy, least of all the squirrel.

Theory aside, your manager's real objectives for the Performance Review are:

- Make you work like a Roman orchard slave.°

- Obtain a signed confession of your crimes against productivity.

- Justify your low salary.

Your objective as an employee is to bilk as much unearned money as possible out of the cold, oppressive entity that masquerades as an employer while it sucks the life-force out of your body.

Luckily for you, I'm on your side.

This chapter will teach you how to glide through the Performance Review process while lining your pockets with the money that rightfully belongs to your more productive co-workers. (If your co-workers have a problem with that, let 'em buy their own helpful book.)

°I don't know if there were any such things as Roman orchard slaves. But if there were, the job probably involved climbing rickety ladders where anybody could look up your toga.

The key to your manager's strategy is tricking you into confessing your shortcomings. Your boss will latch on to those shortcomings like a pit bull on a trespasser's buttocks. Once documented, your "flaws" will be passed on to each new boss you ever have, serving as justification for low raises for the rest of your life. Here are two examples of employees who wandered into that trap:

From E-mail . . .

From: (name withheld)
To: scottadams@aol.com

Scott,

At my company we have to fill out evaluation forms. One has a number of categories (creativity, initiative, teamwork, etc.) with spaces for you to indicate "strengths" and "growth opportunities."

I'm new and didn't know better, so I filled it out honestly, and tried to identify some good growth opportunities. But a co-worker stopped me and said any "growth opportunities" are then automatically spit back to employees by management as examples of poor performance. I don't need any of that, since I'm already the United Way campaigner, and we know what that means.

From: (name withheld)
To: scottadams@aol.com

Scott,

I used to work for [company] doing project management. As a part of that job, I was asked, "What do you think of pie charts?" to which I responded, "Personally, I hate them." I was asked this, in this way, several times by various "superiors."

When I got my next review, I got several negative comments about how I "refused to do pie charts." I pointed out to my boss that I had never been ASKED to do pie charts, merely about my opinion of them. This of course made no difference in my review—"refused to do pie charts" is PART OF MY PERMANENT RECORD!

Your only defense against your boss's "development trap" is to identify development needs in yourself that don't sound so bad:

- "I need to become less attractive so co-workers are not constantly distracted."

- "In the interest of teamwork, I need to learn to control my immense intelligence in the presence of less gifted co-workers."

- "I need to learn how to relax instead of working my typical nine-teen-hour days."

- "I need to make contact with an alien civilization, since their technology is the only thing I don't already understand."

STRATEGY FOR PERFORMANCE REVIEWS

You know you deserve more money than you're getting, based on two undeniable facts:

1. You show up most of the time.

2. See number one.

Your manager might not see it that way (the bastard!). Luckily you have several things working in your favor: (1) Your manager is probably too lazy to write your Performance Review without your "input," and (2) your manager fears that you might cry publicly or resort to violence. Those advantages provide enough traction to pull the "performance train" in your direction.

WRITING YOUR OWN PERFORMANCE REVIEW

Your boss will ask you to document your accomplishments as input for your Performance Review. To the unprepared employee, this might seem like being forced to dig one's own grave. But after studying this chapter you will come to view it more like a jewelry store fantasy.

JEWELRY STORE FANTASY

Imagine your boss as a wealthy but clueless jewelry store owner. He gives you these instructions before leaving for a long vacation. "When nobody's around, count up how many rubies are in that huge sack in the back. I've wondered about that for years."

Performance Reviews can be like a big bag of uncounted rubies. It doesn't matter how many rubies were originally in the bag; what matters is the number you report to your boss. Follow that simple philosophy when describing your accomplishments.

TIPS ON DESCRIBING YOUR ACCOMPLISHMENTS

1. Some people will foolishly limit their list of accomplishments to projects that they've actually worked on. This is a mistake. Don't forget the intangible benefit of "thinking about" a project.

2. No matter how badly your project screwed up, focus on how much money would have been lost if you'd done something even stupider. Then count the difference between the failure you cre-

ated and the even bigger failure you *could* have created as a "cost avoidance."

3. Acronyms are your allies. They sound impressive while conveying no information. Use them liberally.

Boss: "What was your contribution to the project?"

You: "Mostly QA. I was also an SME for the BUs."

Boss: "Um . . . okay. Excellent work."

4. If all you did this year was sit in your cubicle and masturbate, dress it up with the latest buzzwords. Say you're a self-starter who proactively reengineered your personal inventory with Total Quality, conforming to all EEO, OSHA, and ISO 9000 requirements. Stress your commitment to continue this good work into the next fiscal year.

5. Include testimonials from unverifiable sources. Your manager is far too lazy to verify your sources. And since your employee file is confidential, the person you quote doesn't need to know about it either.

6. For this year's accomplishments include everything you did last year and everything you plan to do next year. Bosses don't have a keen grasp of time. If they did, they wouldn't ask you to do six months of work in two weeks. This is your chance to use that curious time-awareness deficiency of your boss to your advantage.

7. Include as your accomplishments anything done by an employee who has a similar name or similar appearance to you. It's worth a shot, and if you're discovered just say, "I always get us confused" and quickly change the subject.

SETTING THE STAGE

You can set the stage for your Performance Review by talking about your accomplishments in glowing terms at every opportunity. Follow this model:

SURROUND YOURSELF WITH LOSERS

Make sure you work in a group with losers. Losers are the ones who will get low raises, thus leaving ample budget funds for you. The worst mistake you could make is to work in a group with highly qualified people. That's a no-win situation for all of you. Losers are your friends (figuratively speaking). If you don't have any losers in your group, help your boss recruit some, preferably in areas that don't affect your life. You want the losers to be within the same general budget area, but not close enough to annoy you on a daily basis.

I remember many joyous occasions after a reorganization at companies where I worked. I would run to get a copy of the new organization chart, almost skipping with joy at the prospect of identifying the co-workers who would "fund" my next raise. Discovering an incompetent co-worker in your group is like finding a gold nugget in your flower garden. It's free money without the burden of additional work.

So if you think the only value that morons provide to the world is to support the commemorative plate industry, you're wrong; they also help pay your salary. You have to respect that.

360-DEGREE REVIEW

If you're lucky enough to have a "360-degree review" process at your company, this is your chance to threaten your boss with "mutually assured destruction." Under this type of system each employee gets to review subordinates, co-workers, and (here's the best part) devil-spawned bosses.

The secret to making this system work for you is to be sure you're the *last* person to complete your review forms. Carry the forms with you wherever you go, occasionally taking them out and saying things like "That reminds me . . ." in the most ominous voice you can muster.

And don't forget to hammer your co-workers too. Every dollar that goes to a co-worker is a dollar that's not available in the budget for you. You might feel selfish doing this, but remember, your co-workers will just blow the money on stupid stuff like education and health care, whereas you would stimulate the economy by spending it on clothes. You have to look at the big picture when you decide how your co-workers "performed."

WRITING YOUR OWN ACCOMPLISHMENTS

Your boss will mentally scale back whatever wild claims you make about yourself on your input to the Performance Review. Fortunately your boss is "flying blind" with no way of knowing how much to scale back.

Therefore, logically, your best strategy is to lie like a shoe salesman with a foot fetish.*

Here are some recommended phrases that I've used as the input for my Performance Reviews over the years, grouped by trendy category. These are written for the boss's signature, thus removing the need for your boss to do any thinking whatsoever.

Does employee demonstrate teamwork?

Scott loves his peers like he loves himself, except without the intense physical attraction. If there's a team, Scott's on it, even if only in spirit or simply taking credit. That's the kind of team player he is.

Does employee have communication skills?

Scott is fluent in seventeen languages including the African one with the clicking sound, which he combines with Morse code in order to multi-task.

Does employee demonstrate customer focus?

Nobody focuses on customers more intensely than Scott. Sometimes it makes the customers nervous, especially the women, but we think they like it.

Does employee demonstrate leadership skills?

Scott is a natural leader. People follow him everywhere he goes, and they watch him too. Some people say Scott is paranoid, but no, that's leadership.

---

*I believe that all shoe sales people have foot fetishes, for the simple economic reason that they'd be willing to work for less pay than somebody who hates feet. That explains why they often "forget" your foot measurement and insist on doing it again.

Does employee model and foster ethical behavior?

Oh yeah. Big time. For example, he would never exaggerate his accomplishments in an attempt to unethically inflate his salary to the level of "market comparables" that he keeps hearing about.

Does employee set high expectations and standards?

Scott's standards are so high that he despises the worthless laggards around him—the so-called co-workers. He thinks even less of the customers, who apparently haven't taken the time to do any comparison shopping.

Scott's expectations are very high. He has often expressed his goal of evolving into pure energy and becoming the supreme overlord of the universe. He's got a long way to go, but his hair loss is a sure sign of some sort of rapid acceleration.

Does employee involve and empower others?

Scott empowers those around him by giving them his work whenever his co-workers are not—in his opinion—busy enough. Sometimes he gives all his work away and has to make up a few things just so everybody gets something. His co-workers couldn't be happier about it because they feel empowered.

Does employee set priorities?

Scott knows his priorities. When I (his feeble and unattractive boss) asked him to work on this Performance Review he hung up the phone on his primary customer and sprang to the keyboard like a panther.

Does employee understand the company vision?

Scott is the only person who has actually "seen" the company vision. He claims it appeared to him one night in the forest and it's "difficult to explain" but he knows it when he sees it. He also came back with some "commandments" from God carved on a flat rock.

(On an unrelated note, Scott has excellent penmanship, based on the observation that it is almost exactly like God's!)

Performance Summary

Scott is my role model. It is my dream to be more like him. Sometimes I follow him around and buy the same clothes. Once in a while I rummage through his trash.

I once observed Scott walking across a lake to heal an injured swan.

He is love.

CONCLUSION

If all else fails, try a subscription to *Soldier of Fortune* magazine and have it delivered to the office. You don't have to read it, just leave it prominently on your desk. Add to your boss's nervousness by asking for "time off to work through a few personal problems."

If you follow my advice, it is my opinion that your next Performance Review will result in a larger raise than you could possibly be worth.

8

PRETENDING TO WORK

When it comes to avoiding work, it's fair to say I studied with the masters. After nine years at Pacific Bell I learned just about everything there was to know about *looking* busy without actually *being* busy. During that time the stock price of Pacific Bell climbed steadily, so I think I can conclude that my avoidance of work was in the best interest of the company and something to be proud of.

Here for the first time ever I am revealing my secrets for Pretending to Work. It's your ticket to freedom.

Your boss is the biggest obstacle to workday leisure. He will try to make you work right up to—but not beyond—the point of death. This may seem like an unfair generalization, because obviously it's more economical for him to push the people who are approaching retirement age a little bit harder.

As an employee, you need a strategy for survival. You need to develop your ability to appear productive without actually expending time or energy. Your very life is at stake.

Based on my painstaking research* I have concluded that there are three types of employees:

1. Those who work hard regardless of the compensation (Idiots).

2. Those who avoid work, thus appearing lazy (Idiots).

3. Those who avoid work while somehow appearing to be productive (Contented Employees).

The rest of this chapter outlines specific strategies for becoming a Contented Employee at the expense of your employer who doesn't deserve somebody as nice as you anyway.

BE A CONSULTANT ON A TEAM

If you can't be a manager, the next best way to avoid real work is to be an "adviser" to people who are doing real work. You might need to develop

*There wasn't much of it, but it hurt.

some actual expertise to become an adviser, but don't go overboard with it. You only need to know one percent more than the people you're advising and then you'll be indistinguishable from Marilyn vos Savant.*

To demonstrate my point, consider this hypothetical situation: You're having a conversation with Albert Einstein and he suddenly gets struck by lightning. This freak accident makes him instantly twice as smart. Could you tell the difference?

Once a person is smarter than you, it doesn't matter if he's one percent smarter or one thousand percent smarter. You can't tell the difference. Don't waste your time acquiring a bunch of knowledge that will do nothing to elevate your perceived value.

The best areas in which to become an expert are those areas that are vital to many projects, shallow in substance, and spectacularly uninteresting. Select an area that is so dry that when the average person is exposed to it he'll want to drill a hole in his head to let the boredom out. Some suggested areas that fit this description:

1. Facilities management

2. Database administration

3. Tax law

WAITING FOR SOMETHING

Seek out assignments that depend heavily on the input of incompetent co-workers, overworked managers, and lying vendors. If any one of them screws up, you won't have the resources you need to do your job. You'll have no choice but to wait around. You can encourage these failures on the part of other people by asking for the things that are least likely to happen:

---

*Marilyn vos Savant has the highest recorded IQ of any human. She once solved a Rubik's Cube just by scaring it into alignment.

- Ask illiterate "outdoorsy" managers to review huge documents in detail.

- Place orders for "vaporware" products that will be "available soon" according to the vendor.

- Ask for meetings with co-workers who have poor time-management skills.

These activities have the unmistakable air of being necessary while at the same time providing you with all the free time you'd ever want.

CHANGE JOBS FREQUENTLY

Job descriptions are hideously cumulative. The longer you stay in one job, the more work you'll be asked to do. That's because people will figure out what you do and they'll know how to find you. Worse yet, you will become competent over time, and that's as good as begging for more work.

Change jobs as often as possible. That clears the deck of all the pesky people who have your phone number. You can then reinvent yourself in a less busy role as an "adviser" to something. Two years is the most you should ever spend in the same job.

COMPLAIN CONSTANTLY ABOUT YOUR WORKLOAD

Take every opportunity to complain about the unreasonable demands that are being placed on you. Reinforce your message during every interaction with a co-worker or manager. Here are some time-tested phrases that you should insert into every conversation:

"I'm up to my ass in alligators."

"I've been putting out fires all day."

"I had fifteen hundred voice mail messages today. Typical."

"It looks like I'll be here on the weekend *again*."

Over time, these messages will work themselves into the subconscious of everybody around you and they will come to think of you as a hard worker without ever seeing a scrap of physical evidence to support the theory.

In other words, don't be this guy:

VOICE MAIL

Never answer your phone if you have voice mail. People don't call you just because they want to give you something for nothing—they call because they want *you* to do work for *them*. That's no way to live. Screen all your calls through voice mail.

If somebody leaves a voice mail message for you and it sounds like impending work, respond during your lunch hour when you know the caller won't be there. That sends a signal that you're hardworking and conscientious even though you're being a devious weasel.

If you diligently employ the method of screening incoming calls and then returning calls when nobody is there you greatly increase the odds that the caller will give up or look for a solution that doesn't involve you. The sweetest voice mail message you can ever hear is "Ignore my last message. I took care of it."

If your voice mailbox has a limit on the number of messages it can hold, make sure you reach that limit frequently. One way to do that is to never erase any incoming messages. If that takes too long, send yourself a few messages. Your callers will hear a recorded message that says "Sorry, this mailbox is full"—a sure sign that you are a hardworking employee in high demand.

If you wake up in the middle of the night to heed nature's call, take a moment to leave a voice mail message for your boss. Your message will automatically leave a recorded time-stamp, thus reinforcing the illusion that you work around the clock. This is a big improvement over reality— that you chugged a beer before going to bed.

Some voice mail systems will activate your pager automatically when a message is left for you. And some voice mail systems will let you schedule a message to be sent at a future time. (I'll bet you know where this is going.) If you have a useless meeting coming up, program the voice mail system to send yourself a voice mail message during the meeting, thus activating your pager. Leave the pager on "beep" instead of vibrate so everybody knows you're being paged. Get a look of horror on your face as you check the incoming number on the pager, then excuse yourself rapidly. Mumble "Ohmygod . . ." on the way out.

ARRIVING AND LEAVING

Always arrive for work before your boss arrives. If you can't do that, leave work after your boss leaves. If you get to work before your boss does you can claim you got there at four A.M. and there's no way to disprove it. If you leave after your boss leaves you can claim you worked until midnight.

Your co-workers are the only ones who can bust you. That's why it's important to let them know that you're watching their arrival and departure times too. That's how you keep one another "honest."

MESSY DESK

Executives can get away with having a clean desk. For the rest of us, it looks like you're not working hard enough. Build huge piles of documents around your work space. To the observer, last year's work looks the same as today's work; it's volume that counts. Pile them high and wide. If you know somebody is coming to your cubicle, bury the document you'll need halfway down in an existing stack and rummage for it when she arrives.

ARRIVAL AND DEPARTURE AT MEETINGS

Come to meetings late and leave early. This leaves the impression that you are so busy you can't do everything. The first part of a meeting is useless and the last part of a meeting is when the assignments are handed out. That is wasted time for a busy person such as yourself.

STUDY THINGS

Get a job that lets you "analyze" or "evaluate" something as opposed to actually "doing" something. When you evaluate something you get to criticize the work of others. If you "do" something, other people get to criticize *you*.

Often there are no clear performance standards for the job of analyzing something. You can take your time, savoring the mistakes of those people who were foolish enough to "do" something.

WORK ON LONG-RANGE PROJECTS

You can easily hide your laziness when you're associated with a long-range project. There's always another day to do the stuff you don't do today. And realistically, the project will probably get canceled or altered beyond recognition before it's completed anyway—so there's no harm done if you don't do your part.

Avoid short-term projects at all costs. They're trouble. People expect results and they expect you to work late to meet deadlines. You don't need that hassle.

LOOKING INCOMPETENT

Nothing is more effective for deflecting work than sheer incompetence. The more incompetent you seem, the less work you'll be asked to do. This is not without its risks, as you might imagine. For example, you might be recognized as an imbecile and promoted into a management job. But short of that risk, it's a pretty safe strategy.

AVOIDING MEANINGLESS ASSIGNMENTS

The average boss generates many meaningless tasks for the employees. Most of the meaningless assignments go to people who are unfortunate enough to fall into one of these categories:

- The person who sits closest to the boss's office.

- The first person who asks a related question.

- The next person who enters the boss's office.

You should never under any circumstances inquire about something that is not part of your job description. Your questions will be interpreted as interest in taking on new work. By virtue of asking the question you become elevated to the position "most appropriate" for any meaningless assignment in that area.

In the boss's eyes, the hapless subordinate whose office is closest will appear like a huge "out basket." Avoid the "out basket" office location even if you have to sleep with the facilities planner to do it.* It's a prison sentence. Every time you hear footsteps you'll have to pretend you're working. Every piddling task ends up on your chair with a little yellow sticky note from the boss. Your value to the corporation will become associated with a stream of unimportant assignments. Your career can never recover from a bad office location.

Never enter the boss's office unless it's absolutely necessary. Every boss saves one corner of the desk for useless assignments that are doled out like Halloween candy to each visitor. Conduct all your business with your boss by voice mail or e-mail, thereby avoiding the "treats" afforded to less clever visitors.

STRATEGIC VACATION PLANNING

Lastly, save some of your vacation for a time when you can use it strategically.

*This is another excellent reason for entering the facilities management profession.

9

SWEARING

THE KEY TO SUCCESS FOR WOMEN

For men, swearing can help them bond with other men. But this contributes in only a tiny way to business success. Men are expected to swear, so it means little when they do. There is no shock value.

For example, if a man comes to the office of another man and offers to show him a report, a typical response might be "Ah, shove it up your ass and die."

Then both men laugh and spit and make passing references to "hooters," thus creating a lifelong bond that cannot be broken.* It's not pretty, but swearing has its place among men, albeit a minor one.

For women it's very different. Swearing can be shocking and attention-grabbing. It is a sign of female power and a disregard for boundaries. And it is the second most important factor for success.

*Unless hooters are involved.

Female Success Factors

1. Who you know

2. Swearing

3. Education

4. What you do

I have reached this conclusion after observing an admittedly small sample of successful female executives who swear like wounded* pirates.

But it's not my fault that the sample size was small. I blame the "glass ceiling." And I take no personal responsibility for the glass ceiling, having spent all of my corporate career under the "glass carpet." Don't get me started.

To understand how swearing can help women, consider the following hypothetical situations:

SCENARIO #1 (WITHOUT SWEARING)

A man comes to a woman's office and offers to show her a report. The woman responds by saying, "Well, I'm a bit busy right now." Undeterred by this mild rebuff, the man will pull up a chair and proceed to chew up an hour of the woman's valuable time. Eventually the woman's productivity will be devoured by an endless parade of men who would rather talk to her than do work. Her career will begin a death spiral, until eventually she becomes a bag lady. And if she doesn't learn to swear, she won't be much of a bag lady either.

Now let's assume that this same woman was adept at the business art of swearing. The scenario might go like this:

---

*And I'm not talking about a flesh wound. I'm talking about the kind where you start shopping for the peg leg and you have to kill your parrot because he won't stop doing Woody Woodpecker jokes.

SCENARIO #2 (WITH SWEARING)

A man comes to a woman's office and offers to show her a report. The woman responds by saying, "Ah, shove it up your ass and die."

The man will be momentarily stunned. It is unlikely that he will pull up a chair. Nor will he experience any bonding. He will probably back slowly out the door. The woman's productivity will skyrocket.

But what about repercussions? The woman might someday need a favor from the man she has just verbally abused. Fortunately for her, all men are trained at birth to accept verbal abuse from women and get over it rather quickly.

And in the unlikely event that the man shows some hesitation to be helpful in the future, the situation can be smoothed over with the simple communication technique of saying, "Do it now or I'll rip off your nuts and shove them down your throat."

There are three scenarios I've left out, but they can be discussed easily:

ACTION	RESULT
Man swears at woman	Six-year prison sentence
Woman swears at woman	How would I know?
Person swears at computer	Improved operation

1 0

HOW TO GET YOUR WAY

This chapter contains strategies to help you get your way. These aren't the kinds of strategies that will propel you to the top of the corporate pig pile, but if you use them you might get some small satisfaction from thwarting the dolts who surround you.

The good thing about dolts is that they can be easily duped. I'll address that issue in more detail in the sequel to this book, titled *Hey, Why'd I Buy Another One of These Books?*

Winning isn't the most important thing in business. You also have to get rich, otherwise there isn't much point to the whole thing. If wealth is all you care about, I recommend becoming a butler for an aging millionaire who has lost his cognitive abilities but not his penmanship. But if you can't be rich, the next best thing is to be smug and cynical. That's where these strategies can help.

THE FINAL SUGGESTION MANEUVER

For years I employed the "Final Suggestion Maneuver" in meetings in which I knew that opinions would vary and that only my own opinion had any value. In other words, I used it in every meeting I ever attended. The success rate of this approach is nothing short of astonishing. And it's a good thing, because the "less than astonishing" zone contains a lot of strategies you don't want to try.

Less Than Astonishing Strategies

- Pretend to be a wax statue.

- Make your own neckties out of toilet seat protectors.

- Use racial epithets to "get people's attention."

- Practice chiropractic arts in your cubicle.

In contrast to those "go nowhere" strategies, the Final Suggestion Maneuver can work for you. It works like this.

Final Suggestion Maneuver

1. Let everybody else make moronic suggestions.

2. Stay uninvolved while the participants shred each other's suggestions like crisp cabbage in a Cuisinart. Watch as they develop intense personal dislikes that will last their entire careers.

3. Toward the end of the allotted meeting time, when patience is
    thin and bladders are full, offer your suggestion. Describe it as
    a logical result of the good thoughts you've heard at the meet-
    ing, no matter how ridiculous that might be.

If you time it right, all the participants will be feeling a sense of incredi-
ble frustration and physical discomfort and will realize that your suggestion is the fastest way to end the horror of the meeting. By disguising your
suggestion as a composite of the participants' thoughts you minimize their
need to attack you to defend their hard-argued positions.

You'll look like the rational deal-maker while the other participants look
like partisan whiners. The only downside is that you won't be singularly
identified with the idea if it works. But that's typically not a problem, since
most ideas don't work. And your boss takes credit for the ones that do.

USE SARCASM TO GET YOUR WAY

By definition, people with bad ideas cannot be swayed by logic. If they
were logical they wouldn't have bad ideas in the first place—unless the
ideas were based on bad data. That leaves you with two possible strategies
for thwarting an illogical idea and getting your way:

*   Argue with data. Do exhaustive research to demonstrate the flaws
    in the person's assumptions.

*   Use sarcasm to mock the idea and make the person look like a
    dolt.

If the "exhaustive research" option looks good to you, you have way too
much time on your hands. Plus, it can only work if you're dealing with a
co-worker who is logical and willing to admit error. And while you're at it,
why not find a co-worker who is an omnipotent supermodel. (Note the
clever use of sarcasm to show the folly of this approach.)

Option two—sarcasm—is more flexible. It works whether the person you wish to manipulate has bad data or a bad brain. Appeal to the person's sense of fear and insecurity. Use sarcasm to point out the potential for future ridicule.

An example will be useful. Let's say that your idiot boss has just suggested that hardworking employees should be rewarded with a certificate of appreciation. Here's how you can use sarcasm to make him change his plans.

EXAMPLE OF THE POWER OF SARCASM

You: "I used to think that all of the problems with our company were caused by poor management and an inadequate compensation system."

Boss: "That's a common misperception."

You: "Now I realize that we were suffering from a shortage of certificates."

Boss: "Um . . ."

You: "The part I like most is that for every person who gets a certificate there will be fifty people who don't—and that spells "extra effort"!"

Boss: "I think I see what you're trying to—"

You: *"I want to earn that certificate! I'll stop at nothing!"*

Boss: "Okay, point made . . ."

You: "Would it be okay if I stayed late tonight and waxed the tables in the conference rooms with my hair?"

THE BIG PICTURE MANEUVER

The theory behind the Big Picture Maneuver is that all white-collar workers are striving to be the one who can see the "big picture" while all those around them are myopic losers. Your co-workers will try to one-up any "big picture" scenario that you lay out. You can manipulate them by taking advantage of that impulse.

Let's say you've just blown a million dollars on a project that went down harder than a drunken ninety-year-old woman with a broken hip. You're sitting in a meeting with a bunch of vultures who would like to spend the entire meeting rubbing your face in the fiscal entrails. Your mission is to escape this fate, and—with luck—even enhance your position. Here's where the Big Picture Maneuver is indispensable.

The conversation might go something like this:

You: "I spent a million dollars but the project didn't work out."

Wally: "You blew a *million dollars*!!"

Alice: "What were you thinking?"

Ted: "Helloooo!!! Wasn't *anybody* managing that thing???"

You: (Coolly looking at the big picture) "A million dollars is just "noise" when you consider the entire Research and Development budget. We're in a risky business."
(At this point the other meeting participants will realize they have been flanked by the Big Picture Maneuver and they will scramble to compensate.)

Wally: "For only a million dollars, we learned a great deal."

Alice: "Compared to the total domestic GNP, it's a rounding error."

Ted: "Can we talk about something *important* now?"

DINOSAUR STRATEGY

The Dinosaur Strategy involves ignoring all new management directives while lumbering along doing things the same way you've always done them.

What makes this strategy successful is that it usually takes six months for your boss to notice your rebellion and get mad about it. Coincidentally, that's about the length of time any boss stays in the same job.

The average life of an organization chart is six months. You can safely ignore any order from your boss that would take six months to complete. In other words, the environment will change before you have to do anything. You can just keep chewing leaves and scampering in the volcanic ash while new bosses come and go.

If you wait long enough, any bad idea will become extinct. And most good ideas too. So if you have time to master only one strategy, this is the one for you.

Example of the Dinosaur Strategy

From: (name withheld)
To: scottadams@aol.com

Scott,

Management, when faced with a management problem, having no clue what to do, but feeling that they should be doing SOMETHING, always seems to resort to the dreaded DATABASE. Of course, they have no strategic plans for actually USING the database, but the activity of putting one together seems to keep them occupied and out of the engineers' hair (for a while).

The first memo explains how the new database will solve all our problems.

The next memo explains that the database is a major corporate undertaking and will require the cooperation of everyone to "shape the vision of the future."

The next few memos explain that the database is still in progress and is looking better and better.

The next memos provide example outputs of what the database will provide, with a disclaimer noting that the data are not yet complete enough to provide meaningful results.

More memos explain that the data collection is taking longer than expected, because the engineers are not providing their inputs in a timely manner.

The engineers continue to ignore all the memos and chastising.

Eventually, all goes quiet and the DATABASE fades into the sunset.

MARKETING AND COMMUNICATIONS

I can speak with some authority on the subject of marketing because I once took a marketing class. Moreover, I have purchased many items.

To an outsider, the entire discipline of marketing might seem like it could be summarized by the following concept:

> If you lower the price you can sell more units.

But this is a gross oversimplification that insults marketing professionals and ignores hundreds of years of cumulative understanding about the subtle intricacies of the marketing arts. Those subtle intricacies are:

- If you raise the price you will sell fewer units.

- How do I look in this outfit?

The Marketing Department uses many advanced techniques to match products and buyers in a way that maximizes profits. For example, they give away keychains.

But that's not all. For your convenience I have summarized the major concepts of marketing so you won't have to sit through a marketing class as I did. You're welcome.

MARKET SEGMENTATION

Every customer wants to get the best product at the lowest price. Fortunately, many customers can't tell the difference between fine Asian silk and Bounty paper towels. No matter how pathetic your product is, there's always somebody who can't tell the difference or won't have access to the alternatives. The job of marketing is to identify these "segments," stick a vacuum pump in their pockets, and suck until all you get is lint.

Market segmentation might sound like a complicated thing, but it's the same process you used as a child to select players for a team. Each potential player is evaluated on objective characteristics, such as speed, skill, and power. If those characteristics don't produce a conclusive choice, then the group is further segmented by their levels of acne and popularity. The children who rate high in the preferred characteristics are placed in the "team segment" and those who rate lowest become the market segment most likely to grow up and purchase inflatable women. It's that simple.

The most important market segment is known as the "Stupid Rich," so named because of their tendency to buy anything that's new regardless of the cost or usefulness. If you can sell enough units to the Stupid Rich, your production costs per unit will decrease. Then you can lower your prices and sell to the Stupid Poor—that's where the real volume is.

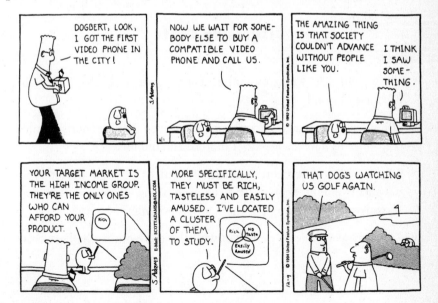

It's never a good idea to design your product for the Smart Poor or the Smart Rich. The Smart Poor will figure out a way to steal your product. The Smart Rich will buy your whole company and fire your ass. As a rule, smart people are an undesirable market segment. Fortunately, they don't exist.

PRODUCT DIFFERENTIATION

The best way to differentiate your product is by making it the best one in its class. But there can be only one best product in every class, and if you're reading this book you probably don't work for that company. So we don't need to get into that strategy.

Suppose you sell a product that is exactly like other products on the market, for example, long distance phone service, insurance, credit cards, or home mortgages. You can make your product look special by disguising the true costs and then claiming it's more economical than the alternatives.

Some good techniques for disguising the true cost of your product include:

Disguising Costs

- Link payments to exotic interest rates, such as the Zambian Floating Q Bond.

- Offer discount plans so confusing that even Nostradamus would throw up his hands and say, "I dunno. You tell me."

- Give coupons that are redeemable for prizes through an impossibly inconvenient process that combines the worst elements of scavenger hunts, tax preparation, and recycling.

- Compare your lowest cost plan with the competitor's highest cost plan.

- Offer lease options to people who are bad at math.

- Assess gigantic penalties for customers who miss payments. Once a year, forget to mail the customer a bill.

- Offer steep discounts for initial payments, followed by obscene price increases. Make it difficult for customers to wiggle out after they're caught in your web.

- Sell the product without any of the features that could make it useful, for example, computers without keyboards and RAM.

THE WIN-LOSE SCENARIO OF MARKETING

Sometimes your company has a bad product at a high price. That's when the real magic of marketing comes into play. The focus changes from educating the consumer to thoroughly screwing the consumer.

If you experience any ethical problems in this situation, remember the Marketing Professional's Motto:

"We're not screwing the customers. All we're doing is holding them down while the salespeople screw them."

Thank goodness for the ignorance of your customers. Confusion is your friend. Take advantage of the goodwill created by your competitors and create products that are eerily similar but much worse.

Examples

Somy Walkman
Honduh Accord
Porch 911
Harry Davidson motorcycles
Popsi Cola

ADVERTISING

Good advertising can make people buy your product even if it sucks. That's important, because it takes the pressure off you to make good products. A dollar spent on brainwashing is more cost-effective than a dollar spent on product improvement.

Obviously there's a minimum quality that every product has to achieve. It should be able to withstand the shipping process without becoming unrecognizable. But after the minimums are achieved, it's advertising that makes the big difference.

A good advertising campaign is engineered to fit a precise audience. In particular, there is a huge distinction between what message works for men and what message works for women.

Males are predictable creatures. That makes it easy to craft a marketing message that appeals to them. All successful advertising campaigns that target men include one of these two messages:

1. This product will help you get dates with bikini models.

2. This product will save you time and money, which you'll need if you want to date bikini models.

Compared to simpleminded, brutish men, women are much more intricate and complex. Your advertising message must appeal to women's greater range of intellectual interests and aesthetic preferences. Specifically, your message has to say this:

1. If you buy this product you'll be a bikini model.

Reinforce your message of "quality" by quoting experts who say good things about your product. Some experts will insist on looking at your product before commenting on it; steer clear of those people. You want the type of expert who can be swayed by a free lunch and a pamphlet.

Don't knock yourself out trying to get your expert to give you the ideal quote. In advertising, as in journalism, you can reword people's quotes for readability. In fact, you can create entirely new sentences using any word the expert has ever spoken. Technically, that's still a quote. Many of your finer publications use this method. You can use it too.

Original Literal Quote

"The lack of quality and complete disregard for the market are evident in this product."

Edited Quote

"The quality are evident in regard of dis product."

UNDERSTANDING THE CUSTOMER

It's essential that you understand the customer. It won't change anything about your product—since those decisions are driven by internal politics—but it's necessary if you want to exhibit an "I'm-more-customer-focused-than-thou" attitude in meetings.

BUILD A BETTER LIFE BY STEALING OFFICE SUPPLIES Dogbert's Big Book of Business 63

The process for understanding customers primarily involves sitting around with other marketing people and talking about what you would do if you were dumb enough to be a customer. It sounds like this:

Marketer #1: "You and I might prefer beef in our hamburgers, but the average consumer isn't that discriminating."

Marketer #2: "I heard of a guy who eats light bulbs and nails."

Marketer #1: "Exactly. They don't care what they eat."

Marketer #2: "So we could fill our burgers with lawn clippings and toenails and that kind of [expletive deleted] and they'd never know the difference."

Marketer #1: "They might even thank us for saving them money."

Marketer #2: "I'm exhausted from all of this market analysis. You want to get a steak?"

Marketer #1: "I'm a vegetarian."

If you've ever actually met a customer, generalize about the behavior of all customers from that one example. If you haven't met a customer, retell the story you heard from somebody who has met a customer, adding your own little twists when absolutely necessary.

Over time, the one customer anecdote will be retold and altered just enough to become "common knowledge" about customer preferences.

True story: A customer for a large phone company complained because he didn't have a way to test his equipment on the public data network unless he paid for the service first. With each telling of this customer's complaint it became obvious that "many customers" needed to test equipment. One manager frequently referred to the "stack of requests" on his desk. Eventually the customer demand became so great that a low-ranking employee was assigned the project of building a multimillion-dollar lab facility to solve the problem. But every time he tried to verify the huge customer demand, each story traced back to the one original guy, who had long since solved his problem. The employee was ordered to build the lab anyway under the theory that there must be more customers like the one guy who asked for it. The project was eventually killed for political reasons. The low-ranking employee eventually left the phone company and became a syndicated cartoonist.

You can use Focus Groups to narrow the range of your research. Focus Groups are people who are selected on the basis of their inexplicable free time and their common love of free sandwiches. They are put in a room and led through a series of questions by a trained moderator.

For many of these people it will be the first time they've ever been fed and listened to in the same day. This can cause some strange behavior. They will begin to complain vehemently about things that never really bothered them before. Then they will suggest product features that they would never buy.

Person #1: "If my toothbrush had a dog brush on the other end I could clean my teeth and brush my Chihuahua at the same time. Now that's a product I'd buy."

Person #2: "Yes, yes! And it could have a third prong for waxing your car at the same time. I'd buy that. If I had a car."

Person #3: "Whoa whoa whoa! What if the toothbrush could also start your car? Or better yet, somebody else's car?"

In time, heady from the thrill of free sandwiches and all the attention, the Focus Group participants will offer breakthrough suggestions that will alter the course of your company forever. Unless you get a bad batch of Focus Group people, in which case they'll eat your sandwiches, bitch about you, and leave.

Now you're ready for market research.

MARKET RESEARCH

In more primitive times, businesses had to use trial and error to find out what customers wanted. That was before market research was invented, thus turning this hodgepodge of guesswork and natural selection into a finely tuned scientific process.

Market research was made possible by the discovery that consumers make rational, well-reasoned buying decisions. That being the case, all you need to do is craft an unbiased survey and ask a statistically valid subset of them what they want.

Here are some of the more successful market research surveys that led directly to the creation of wildly successful products and services that would not have been possible otherwise.

HISTORICAL USES OF MARKET SURVEYS

AIRLINE SURVEY (1920)

If you had to travel a long distance, would you rather:

A. Drive a car.

B. Take a train.

C. Allow yourself to be strapped into a huge metal container that weighs more than your house and be propelled through space by exploding chemicals while knowing that any one of a thousand different human, mechanical, or weather problems would cause you to be incinerated in a spectacular ball of flame.

If you answered "C" would you mind if we stomped on your luggage and sent it to another city?

VCR Survey (1965)

If you could purchase a device that displayed recorded movies on your television, how much would you be willing to pay for it?

A. $200.

B. $500.

C. $2,500 because it will be well worth it if I can rent filthy movies and masturbate like a wild monkey.

Online Computing Survey (1985)

If you could connect your computer to a vast network of information, how would you use this service?

A. Gather valuable scientific information.

B. Improve my education.

C. Demonstrate my complete lack of personality by spending count-less hours typing inane and often obscene sentence fragments that can be viewed by people just like me in "real time."

If you answered "C" above, what should that service be called?

A. Computer Chat.

B. I'm a Moron and I'll Prove It!

C. Good-bye Savings Account.

I GOT A JOB AS THE HEAD OF MARKET RESEARCH AT YOUR COMPANY.
I'LL BE PULLING DOWN $120K PER YEAR.
S. Adams E-Mail: SCOTTADAMS@AOL.COM
I DON'T VALUE OTHER PEOPLE'S OPINIONS SO I'LL JUST USE MY OWN.
7-20
© 1994 United Feature Syndicate, Inc.
JUST FOR REFERENCE, HOW MUCH DOES HONESTY PAY THESE DAYS?
SHUT UP.

IN MARKET RESEARCH TERMS, YOU BELONG TO THE "TECHNO GEEK" SEGMENT.
7-21
S. Adams E-Mail: SCOTTADAMS@AOL.COM
YOU'RE SHY, BORING, GULLIBLE AND MALE. YOU PREFER COMPUTERS TO PEOPLE. THERE'S ALWAYS A SPIDER ON YOUR ARM.
© 1994 United Feature Syndicate, Inc.
MADE YOU LOOK.

I'D LIKE YOUR OPINION FOR MY MARKET RESEARCH, RATBERT.
ME?!!
S. Adams E-Mail: SCOTTADAMS@AOL.COM
I'VE LUMPED YOU IN THE MARKET SEGMENT THAT INCLUDES WILD FUNGI AND PENCIL ERASERS.
7-22
© 1994 United Feature Syndicate, Inc.
QUESTION ONE: WOULD YOU ENJOY HAVING YOUR HEAD RUBBED VIGOROUSLY ON A PIECE OF PAPER?
WHO WOULDN'T?

MARKET REQUIREMENTS

OKAY, LET'S START BY DOCUMENTING YOUR MARKET REQUIREMENTS.
S. Adams E-mail: SCOTTADAMS@AOL.COM
NO, LET'S START BY YOU TELLING ME ALL THE THINGS YOU CAN DESIGN. THEN I'LL TELL YOU WHICH ONE I LIKE.
7/13 © 1995 United Feature Syndicate, Inc. (NYC)
WORK CAN BE VERY REWARDING. YOU SHOULD TRY IT.
WHAT'S THAT DOOHICKEY YOU HAVE THERE?

After you have your market research it's time to design the product. Your engineers will ask you to specify what the product needs to do. That can be a lot of work and it will set you up to take the blame if nobody buys the product later. Avoid specifying market requirements at all costs. If the Engineering Department keeps asking for market requirements, take one of these approaches:

1. Insist that you've already specified the requirements when you said it should be "high quality and low cost." Complain to the engineer's boss that the engineer is stalling.

2. Ask the engineer to tell you all the things that are possible plus the associated cost so you can choose the best solution. Complain to the engineer's boss that the engineer is uncooperative.

3. Specify market requirements that are either technically or logically impossible. Complain to the engineer's boss that the engineer is not being a can-do person.

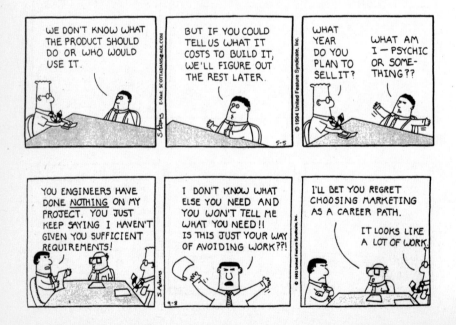

CREATING A MARKET

If there's no market for your product, sometimes you can create one. This involves inventing a problem and then providing the solution. The most effective methods for creating a market include:

PROBLEM YOU CREATE	**MARKET OPPORTUNITY**
Write bad software	Sell upgrades
Build undependable products	Sell service warranties
Tell people they stink	Sell deodorant

NATURAL ENEMIES

Engineers are the natural enemies of marketing people, always trying to inject their unwanted logic and knowledge into every situation. Often they will make unreasonable demands that a product have some use. Sometimes they'll whine endlessly because the product maims customers. If it's not one thing it's another. You can minimize the problem by not inviting them to meetings.

Engineers can be most dangerous when they take advantage of marketing people's tendency to believe whatever they hear, as in these examples:

MARKETING ILLUSTRATED

OUTWARDLY, YES, I'M A RAT. BUT MY BUBBLY PERSONALITY AND MY UTTER LACK OF SKILL MAKE ME WELL-SUITED FOR A CAREER IN MARKETING.
WOULD YOU MIND TERRIBLY IF I GNAWED ON YOUR PHONE CHORD?
WE HAVE AN OPENING IN LOBBY SECURITY.
I'M INSULTED!
E-Mail: SCOTTADAMS@AOL.COM
© 1994 United Feature Syndicate, Inc.
12-14

I'M SORRY, DAVE, BUT YOU'RE BEING TRANSFERRED TO MARKETING AND THERE'S NO BUDGET TO TRAIN YOU AS A MARKETER.
SLAP!
WHERE AM I? I NEED A DRINK.
THIS IS A TEMPORARY FIX... BUT YOU'LL FIT IN NOW.
E-Mail: SCOTTADAMS@AOL.COM
© 1993 United Feature Syndicate, Inc.
1-3-94

IN ADDITION TO MY CURRENT DUTIES, I'LL BE MANAGING THE MARKETING GROUP.
THE MARKETING JOB OPENED BECAUSE THE PREVIOUS MANAGER GOT RUN DOWN IN THE PARKING LOT.
WHEN THEY NEEDED A GOOD MANAGER, THEY KNEW WHERE TO LOOK.
UNDER YOUR BUMPER?
E-Mail: SCOTTADAMS@AOL.COM
© 1994 United Feature Syndicate, Inc.
10-6

I'VE NEVER MANAGED MARKETING PEOPLE BEFORE. BUT A GOOD MANAGER CAN MANAGE ANYTHING.
SO... I ORDER YOU TO GO DO MARKETING THINGS... LIKE SEGMENTING AND FOCUS GROUPS...
AND KEEP ON FOCUSING AND SEGMENTING UNTIL WE DOMINATE THE INDUSTRY!!!
WELL, I'M MOTIVATED.
E-Mail: SCOTTADAMS@AOL.COM
© 1994 United Feature Syndicate, Inc.
10-7

Marketing Antics Reported by E-mail

From: (name withheld)
To: scottadams@aol.com

Scott,

Here's a mind-boggling stupid idea from our Marketing Department that you might be able to use.

We make [type of machine]. A new version of our product is both cheaper and faster. A great breakthrough, right?

Well, Marketing wants Engineering to slow the unit down so they have a low-cost unit to sell. Then sell them upgrades to full speed at an enormous price. These would be physically identical, just one would have the code messed up on purpose to run slow.

From: (name withheld)
To: scottadams@aol.com

Scott,

We asked the Marketing Division to give us some numbers in regard to how many of each product they want to sell.

Their reply: We need "X" number of dollars. You figure out how many of each product you need to produce to meet that figure.

Our conclusion: Marketing has no idea how to do its job; Marketing does not want to do its job; Marketing and related vital business activities (such as forecasting) are all figments of our imagination.

From: (name withheld)
To: scottadams@aol.com

Scott,

Before I started at [company] two years ago, they had completed their base-level product. On the verge of making a couple of sales, Marketing decided to divulge some of the details of
the "next-generation system" to the potential customers. They
all liked the sound of it so much that they decided to *not* buy
the current system and wait for the new one. [Company's]
potential customers are looking for a system that will be put in
place and expected to last as much as twenty-five years, so they
are not going to rush into a purchase.

Three years later the "next-generation" system is almost
done. Customers are impressed with demo units, but express
some reservations.

"Not to worry," says Marketing, "in two years we will have a
'high-performance system' completed which will take care of
your concerns."

Once again, the customers have decided to wait. In the mean-
time, [company] has run out of $$$, and the much-advertised
"high-performance system" is only in the early planning stages.
All the production people have been laid off, but most of the
managers and all of the marketers are still employed. The final
system may never become a reality.

MANAGEMENT CONSULTANTS

THE DOGBERT CONSULTING COMPANY WILL PLOT A NEW COURSE FOR YOUR BUSINESS.

MY CONSULTANTS ARE SO SMART THAT THEIR BRAINS DON'T FIT IN THEIR HEADS. THEY HAVE TO STRAP THE EXTRA BRAINS TO THEIR TORSOS.

WHY DO I NEED A PIECE OF LIVER STRAPPED TO MY TORSO?

I GOT A LITTLE CARRIED AWAY AT THE PITCH MEETING.

If the employees of your company are incompetent you might want to get some consultants. A consultant is a person who takes your money and annoys your employees while tirelessly searching for the best way to extend the consulting contract.

Consultants will hold a seemingly endless series of meetings to test various hypotheses and assumptions. These exercises are a vital step toward tricking managers into revealing the recommendation that is most likely to generate repeat consulting business.

After the "correct" recommendation is discovered, it must be justified by a lengthy analysis. The consultants begin working like crazed beavers in a coffee lake. Reams of paper will disappear. You'll actually be able to hear the screams of old-growth forests dying as the consultants churn out page after page of backup charts and assumptions. The analysis will be cleverly designed to be as confusing as possible, thus discouraging any second-guessing by sniping staff members who are afraid of appearing dense.

When consultants are added to a department they change the balance and chemistry of the group. You need a new process to take advantage of the consultants' skills. The most efficient process is to use the dullard employees as data gatherers to feed the massive brains of the consultants. This keeps the employees busy and makes them feel involved while the consultants hold meetings with senior managers of the company to complain about the support they're getting and to pitch new projects.

Consultants use a standard set of decision tools that involve creating "alternative scenarios" based on different "assumptions." Any pesky assumptions that don't support the predetermined recommendation are quickly discounted as being uneconomical—for the consultants.

The remaining assumptions are objectively validated by sending employees off to obtain information that is not available. Later, the assumptions are transformed into near-facts through the process of sitting around arguing about what is "most likely."

Consultants will ultimately recommend that you do whatever you're *not* doing now. Centralize whatever is decentralized. Flatten whatever is vertical. Diversify whatever is concentrated and divest everything that is not "core" to the business. You'll hardly ever find a consultant who recommends that you keep everything the same and stop wasting money on consultants. And consultants will rarely deal with the root cause of your company's problems, since that's probably the person who hired them. Instead, they'll look for ways to improve the "strategy" and the "process."

Consultants don't need much experience in an industry in order to be experts. They learn quickly. If your twenty-six-year-old consultant drives past the Egghead software outlet on the way to an assignment, that would qualify as experience in the software industry. If Egghead has a sale on modems that day: hardware experience. This type of experience is unavailable to the regular staff members who have worked in the industry for twenty years but still use yellow sticky notes to identify their various excretory openings.

Aside from their massive intellects, consultants bring many advantages to your company that regular employees can't match.

- Consultants have credibility because they are not dumb enough to be regular employees at your company.

- Consultants eventually leave, which makes them excellent scapegoats for major management blunders.

- Consultants can schedule time on your boss's calendar because they don't have your reputation as a whiny little troublemaker who constantly brings up unsolvable "issues."

- Consultants are often more attractive than your regular employees. This is not always true, but if you get a batch of homely ones you can always replace them in a month.

- Consultants will return your calls, because it's all billable time to them.

- Consultants work preposterously long hours, thus making the regular staff feel like worthless toads for working only sixty hours a week.

CONSULTANTS ILLUSTRATED

HERE'S MY FINAL CONSULTING REPORT ON YOUR COMPANY.
S. Adams E-Mail: SCOTTADAMS@AOL.COM
5-14
I'VE LISTED ALL THE DEADWEIGHT EMPLOYEES WHO SHOULD BE FIRED.
© 1994 United Feature Syndicate, Inc.
THIS IS THE COMPANY DIRECTORY.
FINDING THAT WAS A HUGE TIME-SAVER.

I'VE SEEN HIM BEFORE.
I'M A "BLAME CONSULTANT."
S. Adams E-Mail: SCOTTADAMS@AOL.COM
FOR A LARGE FEE I WILL TELL THE WORKERS THAT THE PROBLEMS IN THE COMPANY ARE THEIR FAULT, NOT YOURS. IT'S THE LATEST MANAGEMENT FAD.
9-14
© 1993 United Feature Syndicate, Inc.
WON'T THEY SEE RIGHT THROUGH THAT?
IS THAT MY FAULT??!

DOGBERT IS HIRED AS A BLAME CONSULTANT.
THE COMPANY'S PROBLEMS ARE YOUR FAULT, WILLY.
S. Adams E-Mail: SCOTTADAMS@AOL.COM
YOU BLAME THE SENIOR EXECUTIVES, BUT IT IS YOU — THE INDIVIDUAL EMPLOYEE — WHO MUST BUILD INNOVATIVE NEW PRODUCTS AND PIONEER NEW MARKETS.
9-15
© 1993 United Feature Syndicate, Inc.
BUT I'M JUST A WORD PROCESSOR. I WAS HIRED TO TYPE.
I'VE SEEN YOUR TYPING. THAT STINKS TOO.

DOGBERT IS HIRED AS A BLAME CONSULTANT.
THE COMPANY'S WOES ARE YOUR FAULT, NOT SENIOR MANAGEMENT'S!
9-16
S. Adams E-Mail: SCOTTADAMS@AOL.COM
DO YOU REALIZE HOW MUCH YOU COULD GAIN PERSONALLY BY MAKING THE COMPANY A SUCCESS?
© 1993 United Feature Syndicate, Inc.
I WOULD GET A NICE PLAQUE IN A PLASTIC FRAME.
YEAH... I WAS HOPING YOU DIDN'T KNOW.

HERE'S MY CONSULTING REPORT ON YOUR COMPANY.
9-17
S. Adams E-Mail: SCOTTADAMS@AOL.COM
I HAD NO INSIGHTS SO I BULKED IT UP BY ADDING WITTY ANALOGIES.
© 1993 United Feature Syndicate, Inc.
"HIS HEAD WAS LIKE A HOLLOW PUTTY BALL ATTACKED BY TWO POINTY DUST BUNNIES."
VIVID, ISN'T IT?

MY FEE FOR BUSINESS CON-SULTING IS $200 AN HOUR.
FAIR ENOUGH.
I'LL SPEND THE DAY QUESTIONING YOUR EMPLOYEES TO IDEN-TIFY PROBLEM AREAS.
© 1991 United Feature Syndicate, Inc.
LATER
IT'S UNANIMOUS. THEY'RE UNDER-PAID AND ALL THE PROBLEMS ARE YOUR FAULT, "LARD HEAD."

DOGBERT IS A CONSULTANT
YOUR PROFITS ARE PLUNGING.
$
THE PROB-LEM WILL NOT BE EASY TO SOLVE.
BRAINS
← Competitors
← Beavers
← You
© 1991 United Feature Syndicate, Inc.
SO, WHAT SHOULD WE DO? CUT THE TRAINING BUDGET AGAIN?

DOGBERT IS A CONSULTANT
I HAVE AN UNORTHODOX PLAN FOR IMPROVING YOUR IMAGE IN THE COMPANY.
SHOOT.
© 1991 United Feature Syndicate, Inc.
LUCKY GUESS.

WALLY? I THOUGHT YOU GOT FIRED.
I DID.
BUT PEOPLE OUTSIDE THE COMPANY APPEAR SMARTER. SO THEY HIRED ME BACK AS A CONSULTANT FOR WAY MORE MONEY.
DID YOU UNDERSTAND THAT? DON'T FEEL EMBARRASSED TO ASK FOR HELP ON THE HARD STUFF.
S. Adams
E-Mail: SCOTTADAMS@AOL.COM
10-1
© 1994 United Feature Syndicate, Inc.

GREAT NEWS-- YOU'RE FIRED!
YOU GET A GENEROUS SEVERANCE PACKAGE, TWO WEEKS' VACATION, AND WE HIRE YOU BACK AS A CONTRACTOR FOR MORE MONEY!!
AND I CAN TELECOMMUTE IF I WANT, BUT SINCE DRESS CODES DON'T APPLY TO ME...
AARGH!
Bonk Bonk
S. Adams
E-Mail: SCOTTADAMS@AOL.COM
10-20
© 1994 United Feature Syndicate, Inc.

IT LOOKS LIKE YOU'RE OFF TO A THREE HOUR STAFF MEETING THAT DOESN'T APPLY TO ME.
I'M GLAD I'M A HIGHLY PAID CONTRACTOR. I'LL BE INCREASING MY SKILLS WHILE YOU FIGHT TO GET OXYGEN TO YOUR BRAINS.
THREE HOURS LATER
I BECAME A MULTIMEDIA DEVELOPER. HOW WAS YOUR DAY?
S. Adams
E-Mail: SCOTTADAMS@AOL.COM
10-21
© 1994 United Feature Syndicate, Inc.

AS YOUR CONSULTANT, I'LL TELL YOU HOW TO IMPROVE YOUR BUSINESS PROCESSES.
I'LL SHOW YOU HOW A WELL-DESIGNED PROCESS CAN COMPENSATE FOR YOUR SLOTH, APATHY AND ALL-AROUND INCOMPETENCE.
BUT MOST IMPORTANT: LET'S HAVE FUN.
S. Adams
E-Mail: SCOTTADAMS@AOL.COM
11-10
© 1994 United Feature Syndicate, Inc.

DOGBERT THE CONSULTANT
A GOOD WAY TO JUDGE CORPORATE HEALTH IS TO LOOK AT YOUR EMPLOYEE TURNOVER RATE.
S. Adams E-Mail: SCOTTADAMS@AOL.COM
OUR TURNOVER RATE IS VERY LOW. WE ONLY HIRE PEOPLE WHO AREN'T SKILLED ENOUGH TO WORK ANYPLACE ELSE.
11-21
© 1994 United Feature Syndicate, Inc.
MAYBE METRICS AREN'T THE WAY TO GO HERE.
NO METRIC HAS BEATEN ME YET!!

DOGBERT THE CONSULTANT
YOU CAN GAUGE YOUR SUCCESS BY THE NUMBER OF REPEAT CUSTOMERS YOU HAVE.
S. Adams E-Mail: SCOTTADAMS@AOL.COM
I'M PROUD TO SAY THAT VIRTUALLY EVERY CUSTOMER GETS ANOTHER UNIT WITHIN THREE MONTHS OF BUYING THE FIRST ONE!
11/22
© 1994 United Feature Syndicate, Inc.
WHAT IF YOU DON'T COUNT WARRANTY REPLACE-MENTS?
OOH... THEN WE DON'T LOOK SO GOOD.

DOGBERT IS A CREATIVITY CONSULTANT
HERE'S MY FINAL REPORT ON YOUR COMPANY.
S. Adams © 1993 United Feature Syndicate, Inc.
I'VE CONCLUDED THAT YOU'RE DOOMED. YOU WASTE TOO MUCH MONEY ON CONSULTANTS.
Internet: ScottAdams@AOL.com
YOU'RE A CONSULTANT.
IRONIC, ISN'T IT?

TALES OF CONSULTANTS

From: (name withheld)
To: scottadams@aol.com

Scott,

Here's one that happened at a company I worked for. . . .
President of the company ignores suggestions by employees on how to improve operations. He hires a consultant to come in and make suggestions. Consultant talks to employees, gets their same suggestions, and presents them to president, who says they are "good ideas" and implements them.
Quite irritating, it was. . . .

From: (name withheld)
To: scottadams@aol.com

Scott,

I used to work at a large company that made nuclear weapons and MRI scanners. They hired a consulting group to come in and tell them how they should change the business.
The consultants said that [company name] was the company to be like. That company started a bike business from nothing and had grown to become some huge presence in a very short time.
When you ordered your bike, they measured you and made a bike to your size and painted it the color you wanted. You had it within two weeks. The theme here was customizing to the customer.
We made very large expensive MRI scanners. We weren't sure if that meant we had to paint them different colors.

The middle managers were all toeing the company line and trying to whip us into agreement. At the same time, I was looking for a bike and I thought it would be neat to have one measured for me. I went looking for a [company name] bike, but I couldn't find any. Bicycle shops told me that the bike manufacturer went out of business.

The next day I mentioned it to my manager. He informed me I was naive (I was) and that I must be wrong (I wasn't).

It really pissed me off, so I called some of the shops that had ads with [company name] brand names and got their regional contact. The regional contact said they no longer were in the business and gave me the national contact.

When I called the national contact I got the division that handles "massage and bath products" for [company name]. He said they hadn't been in that business for at least six months and if there was anything left it was sold to [another company name].

I documented all my facts and contacts and phone numbers and went back to confront my manager. (I told you I was naive.) I guess he took it to his manager and that was the last we heard of that.

I bet they never called the numbers.

From: (name withheld)
To: scottadams@aol.com

Scott,

About four months ago, my company [a copy center] hired a very expensive consultant to teach us all about the new "Q Program," the basic upshot of which is that we aren't allowed to make mistakes anymore. Naturally, we raised the question of the possibility of such perfection, and his arguments went something like this:

(A) If you can go for ten seconds without making any mistakes, you can go for a minute without making any mistakes. And if you can go for a minute, you can go for sixty perfect minutes. And so on and so forth.

(B) You're saying it's okay for [company] to make mistakes? How many are okay? One in a hundred? Yes? What if doctors dropped one in a hundred babies on their heads? What if one out of a hundred planes crashed into the side of a mountain?

Yes, the man actually drew a parallel between copying errors and the deaths of thousands.

BUSINESS PLANS

Somewhere between the hallucinations of senior management and the cold reality of the market lies something called a business plan. There are two major steps to building a business plan:

1. Gather information.

2. Ignore it.

In the information-gathering phase, each area of the company is asked to predict its revenues and expenses for the coming years. As you might expect, the predictions will be "padded" to make them easy to achieve. For example, if a business unit sold a million units last year it might submit less aggressive targets for the coming year.

SALES ESTIMATE FOR NEXT YEAR

"Sales will be negative for the year. We expect that many shoplifters will take our product off the shelf and bring it to the cashier for a refund using only gum wrappers as receipts. Medical expenses will be up thirty percent because the few customers who actually pay for our products will return them by throwing them at employees."

Senior management will look at the aggregated lies of the individual business units and adjust them to where they "know they should be." This can cause a fairly large gap between what the employees think they can do and what senior management tells them they must do. This gap can be closed by adjusting the assumptions.

First, assume that any positive trends will continue forever and any negative trends will turn around soon. Then run the numbers through a computer spreadsheet. The result is the future. (Later, if you turn out to be wrong, blame it on the global economy.)

Some companies change what they're doing to get the future they want. This is a waste of time. You can get the same result by adjusting the assumptions in your business plan. Remember, the future depends on assumptions and the assumptions are just stuff you make up. No sense in knocking yourself out.

It is never a good idea to be constrained by reality when you craft your assumptions for the business case. Reality is very unpopular and it is not fun to read. If you've never seen any reality written down, here are some examples to illustrate how unmotivating it can be.

Assumptions Based on Reality (Avoid)

The project team leader is a nitwit. Our best case scenario is that he won't run with tools in his hands and hurt someone.

The project team will need additional people. Management will respond by increasing the frequency of status reports.

Our market research was apparently conducted at a mental health clinic. Either that or there really is a robust market demand by people named Moses.

On the surface it might seem unethical to build a business plan that intentionally avoids any contact with reality. I say "pish tosh" to that, not because it means anything, but just because it's fun to say.*

Everybody knows that business plans are created after decisions have been made by the executives of your company. Therefore, nobody believes your assumptions anyway. So you're not being unethical when you use ludicrous assumptions, you're just lying to keep your job. People will respect you for that.

It's not always easy to craft assumptions that support the result your executives want. But I'm here to help. Here are some valuable tips for getting the "right" answers in your analyses.

---

* Go ahead, try it. You'll find yourself saying pish tosh often and liking it.

Irrational Comparisons

If there's a better solution than the one your executives want you to justify, avoid it like a William Shatner poetry festival. Make no mention of the better alternative and hope nobody notices. Instead, focus on the hideously stupid alternatives that make the recommended approach look good in comparison.

Bad Alternatives That Make Yours Look Good

1.   Upgrade obsolete equipment.

2.   Hire hordes of troublemaking, union-inclined workers.

3.   Do nothing and watch the business crumble while your nimble competitors reap obscene profits, live in big houses, and use your relatives as servants.

UNREALISTIC REVENUE PROJECTIONS

If only one percent of the world buys your product, that's fifty million customers!

Some variation of that "analysis" has been used successfully by every company that ever launched a product. It's a compelling argument for launching a new product because everybody knows that the general population breaks down this way:

> 60%   People who don't need your product
> 30%   People who have no money
> 5%   People who are nuts
> 5%   People who will buy any damn thing

That leaves a neat ten percent of the population who can be considered likely customers for your product, and that's more than enough to support a business plan. If somebody questions your market projections, simply point out that your target market is "People who are nuts" and "People who will buy any damn thing." Nobody is going to tell you there aren't enough of those people to go around.

WRITING THE COMPANY BUSINESS PLAN

Employees want to feel that they participated in the formation of the business plan. This scam is called "buy-in," and it's essential for reminding the employees that if anything goes wrong it's their fault.

These are the important steps to achieving buy-in for a company business plan.

1. Executives set the company direction with useful statements such as "Become the market leader in fabric softener and satellite communications."

   This direction is essential, because employees can easily be misled into believing that the goal of the company is to go out of business. Or worse, a driver for a delivery truck might become confused by the absence of direction and start designing microchip circuits instead of hauling fabric softener.

2. Employees are asked to objectively rank the value of their activities in supporting the company's objectives.

3. Employees rank every activity as a top priority, critical to the very existence of the company. They support their claims with indecipherable, acronym-laden bullet points.

4. The employees' input is collected into large binders.

5. The Budget Department uses the input from the employees as the basis for lengthy discussions about the relative stupidity and worthlessness of each department.

   Eventually, budget recommendations are made on the basis of several weighted factors:

10%	Which project acronyms are most familiar to the Budget Department.
10%	Fourth-hand anecdotes they've heard that would indicate executive support for a particular project.
80%	What department the budget people would like to eventually work in if only they could find a way to get out of doing budgets.

6. A technical writer is called in to accept the blame for the fact that the various components of the plan make no sense and important projects are unfunded. Feeling bitter and cynical, but secure in

the knowledge that nobody will ever see the plan, the technical writer cobbles a document together and then resigns in disgust after erasing the source file.

7. The plan is locked up in a secure place because it is too proprietary to share with the employees.

ENGINEERS, SCIENTISTS, PROGRAMMERS, AND OTHER ODD PEOPLE

People who work in the fields of science and technology are not like other people. This can be frustrating to the nontechnical people who have to deal with them. The secret to coping with technology-oriented people is to understand their motivations. This chapter will teach you everything you need to know.

All technical professionals share a common set of traits. For convenience, I will focus primarily on engineers. It is safe to generalize to the other science and technology professions.

For the record, I'm not an engineer by training. But I spent ten years working with engineers and programmers in a variety of jobs. I learned their customs and mannerisms by observing them, much the way Jane Goodall learned about the great apes, but without the hassle of grooming.

In time, I came to respect and appreciate the ways of engineers. Eventually I found myself adopting their beautiful yet functional philosophies about life. It was too late for me to go back to school and become a real engineer but at least I could pretend to be one and enjoy the obvious benefits of elevated sexual appeal. So far I think it's working.

Engineering is so trendy these days that everybody wants to be one. The word "engineer" is greatly overused. If there's somebody in your life who you think is trying to pass as an engineer, give him this test to discern the truth.

ENGINEER IDENTIFICATION TEST

You walk into a room and notice that a picture is hanging crooked. You . . .

A. Straighten it.

B. Ignore it.

C. Buy a CAD system and spend the next six months designing a solar-powered, self-adjusting picture frame while often stating aloud your belief that the inventor of the nail was a total moron.

The correct answer is "C" but partial credit can be given to anybody who writes "It depends" in the margin of the test or simply blames the whole stupid thing on "Marketing."

My contribution to the understanding of engineers will be to try to explain the noble, well-reasoned motives behind what the so-called normal people perceive as odd behaviors.

SOCIAL SKILLS

It's totally unfair to suggest—as many have—that engineers are socially inept. Engineers simply have different objectives when it comes to social interaction.

"Normal" people expect to accomplish several unrealistic things from social interaction:

- Stimulating and thought-provoking conversation

- Important social contacts

- A feeling of connectedness with other humans

These goals are irrational and stupid. Experience shows that most conversations degenerate into discussions about parking spaces, weather patterns, elapsed time since you last exercised, and—God forbid—"feelings." These topics hardly qualify as stimulating and thought-provoking. Nor are they useful.

Engineers realize that making personal contacts is not valuable in their occupation. For them it's not "who you know" that matters, it's "who knows less than you do" that counts.

Nor is there much tangible value in feeling "connected" with other humans. That stuff is best left to the poets and the multilevel marketing organization. To an engineer, most "normal" people are intellectually indistinguishable from Mexican jumping beans with faces.* Feeling "connected" with carbon-based dolts holds all the joy of being handcuffed to a dead zebra—it sounds special, but it can get old fast.

In contrast to "normal" people, engineers have rational objectives for social interactions:

- Get it over with as soon as possible.

- Avoid getting invited to something unpleasant.

- Demonstrate mental superiority and mastery of all subjects.

These are sensible goals and ones that can produce great joy. The social skill of an engineer must be evaluated on the basis of these rational objectives, not on the basis of bizarre and nonsensical societal standards. Viewed in this light, I think you'll agree that engineers are very effective in their social interactions. It's the "normal" people who are nuts.

FASCINATION WITH GADGETS

To the engineer, all matter in the universe can be placed into one of two categories: (1) things that need to be fixed, and (2) things that will need to be fixed after you've had a few minutes to play with them. Engineers like to solve problems. If there are no problems handily available, they will create their own problems. Normal people don't understand this concept; they believe that if it ain't broke, don't fix it. Engineers believe that if it ain't broke, it doesn't have enough features yet.

No engineer looks at a television remote control without wondering what it would take to turn it into a stun gun. No engineer can take a shower without wondering if some sort of Teflon coating would make

---

*If you think it's easy to come up with great analogies let's see you do it.

showering unnecessary. To the engineer, the world is a toy box full of sub-optimized and feature-poor toys.

That's a good thing, society-wise.

If not for the compulsions of engineers, mankind would have never seen the wheel, settling instead for the trapezoid because some Neanderthal in Marketing convinced everybody it had great braking ability. And there would be no fire, because some middle-manager cave person would point out that if fire was such a good idea the other cave people would already be using it.

From E-mail . . .

> From: (name withheld)
> To: scottadams@aol.com
>
> Scott,
>
> I work for [company] as a tech-rep, providing on-site service to a variety of clients. Once, I answered a call at an engineering firm. They said the copier was jamming. When I got there I discovered a huge pile of copier components, nuts, bolts, etc. and a stripped copier frame.
>
> The head engineer had compiled a two-volume set of notes listing real, false, and perceived faults with the copier. They had recorded time of day, job conditions (one-sided copies, two-sided copies, document handler selected/nonselected, paper weight, etc.), and line voltage fluctuations. I asked them why they had disassembled it, and they replied, "So it would take you less time to fix it."
>
> It took four days (I am not kidding or exaggerating in the least!) to reassemble and set up page after page of meticulous, tedious adjustments.
>
> And do you know what the problem was? They had put developer in the ink receptacle! From a tech-rep's point of view the easiest thing in the world to diagnose, takes thirty minutes to fix (on that particular product).

FASHION AND APPEARANCE

Clothes are the lowest priority for an engineer, assuming the basic thresholds for temperature and decency have been satisfied. If no appendages are freezing or sticking together, and if no genitalia or mammary glands are swinging around in plain view, then the objective of clothing has been met. Anything else is a waste.

If you think about it logically, you are the only person who doesn't have to look at yourself, not counting the brief moments you look in the mirror. Engineers understand that their appearance only bothers other people and therefore it is not worth optimizing.

Another plus: Bad fashion can discourage normal people from interacting with the engineer and talking about the cute things their children do.

LET ME INTRODUCE YOU TO ONE OF OUR ENGINEERS.
KAREN IS OUR NEW VICE PRESIDENT. AND YOU ARE...?
DILBERT: VALUED EMPLOYEE.
I BELIEVE IN OPEN COMMUNICATIONS, DILBERT. FEEL FREE TO TALK ABOUT ANY-THING.
UH-OH
SO, WHAT WERE YOU WORKING ON?
OH-NO
WELL... I WAS JUST SENDING AN E-MAIL TO SOMEBODY WHO SITS BY A WINDOW TO ASK IF IT'S RAIN-ING.
IF IT'S RAINING I'LL FASHION A RAINCOAT FROM A LARGE TRASH BAG.
WATCH.
THREE HOLES AND YOU'RE READY TO GO!
ARE YOU PLANNING TO GO OUT AT LUNCH?
ONLY IF IT RAINS.

DILBERT, I WANT YOU TO INTERVIEW THE JOB APPLICANT WHO'S COMING IN TODAY.
SEE IF HE'S GOT WHAT IT TAKES TO BE AN ENGINEER.
HI, KARL. WE'LL START WITH THE STANDARD ENGI-NEERING TEST.
OKEY-DOKEY.
I HAVE THIRTY-FIVE PENS AND PENCILS HERE. HOW MANY ARE REALLY NEEDED TO PERFORM YOUR JOB?
ALL OF THEM.
CORRECT... NOW, WHAT IS THE PROPER WAY TO CARRY THEM WITH YOU?
RIGHT AGAIN. LAST QUESTION: WHAT IS THE ADVANTAGE OF WEARING NATURAL FABRICS?
UH-OH... PANIC SITUATION.
I... I DON'T KNOW.
THAT'S OKAY. I WAS TESTING YOUR HAIR. YOU'RE AN ENGINEER.

I HAVE TO GIVE A SPEECH TO THE "SOCIETY OF ENGINEERS" TODAY... I'M A BIT NERVOUS.
SOMETIMES YOU CAN RELAX BY IMAGINING THE AUDIENCE IS NAKED.
WHOA! CANCEL THAT. I JUST PICTURED FOUR HUNDRED NAKED ENGINEERS.
TOO LATE.

LOVE OF "STAR TREK"

Engineers love all of the "Star Trek" television shows and movies. It's a small wonder, since the engineers on the starship *Enterprise* are portrayed as heroes, occasionally even having sex with aliens. Every engineer dreams about saving the universe and having sex with aliens. This is much more glamorous than the real life of an engineer, which consists of hiding from the universe and having sex without the participation of other life forms. Consequently, ratings for "Star Trek" will remain high as long as they stay away from any realism.

DATING AND SOCIAL LIFE

Dating is never easy for engineers. A normal person will employ various indirect and duplicitous methods to create a false impression of attractiveness. Engineers are incapable of placing appearance above function.

For society, it's probably a good thing that engineers value function over appearance. For example, you wouldn't want engineers to build nuclear power plants that only *look* like they would keep all the radiation inside. You have to consider the global perspective. But the engineer's emphasis on function over form is a big disadvantage for dating, where the goal is to act phony until the other person loves you for the person that you are.

Engineers don't like to make small talk because no useful information is exchanged. It is more useful to explain complicated technology issues to any human who will stand still. That way at least some information is exchanged and the encounter is not wasted. Unfortunately, it seems that a normal person would rather have a bushel of pine cones rammed up the nose° than listen to a story about technology. But that's no reason to stop imparting valuable knowledge to a person who doesn't want it.

Sometimes normal people will try to use body language to end an encounter with an engineer. But engineers ignore body language because

---

°In controlled lab tests, nineteen out of twenty subjects preferred to have pine cones rammed up their noses. The other subject preferred to have the engineer rammed up his nose. He'll be missed.

it is an imprecise science at best. For example, it's almost impossible to tell the difference between a comatose stare and an expression of interest.

Fortunately, engineers have an ace in the hole. They are widely recognized as superior marriage material: intelligent, dependable, employed, honest, and handy around the house. While it's true that many normal people would prefer not to *date* an engineer, most normal people harbor an intense desire to *mate* with them, thus producing engineerlike children who will have high-paying jobs long before losing their virginity.

Male engineers reach their peak of sexual attractiveness later than normal men, becoming irresistible erotic dynamos in their mid thirties to late forties. Just look at these examples of sexually irresistible men in technical professions:

- Bill Gates.

- MacGyver.

- Etcetera.

Female engineers become irresistible at the age of consent and remain that way until about thirty minutes after their clinical death. Longer if it's a warm day.

BATTLING UNFAIR STEREOTYPES

Engineers are often stereotyped in the media. It is horribly unfair to assign a set of common traits to an entire group of people. There is some talk that I have been guilty of doing this myself, but I contend I've been framed.

To set the record straight, I have interviewed thousands of engineers and determined that the stereotypes do *not* fit them all. Here are the exceptions I found:

ENGINEER	EXCEPTION TO STEREOTYPE
Elmer Moline, Calgary, Canada	Had a second date at age twenty-three
Herb Blinthem, San Jose, California	Enjoyed *Bridges of Madison County*
Anita Fluman, Dublin, California	Has rhythm
Hugh Hunkelbein, Schaumburg, Illinois	Doesn't care how his television remote control works as long as it does

I JOINED THE "SCIENTIST ANTI-DEFAMATION LEAGUE."
WHAT'S THAT?
THEY FIGHT AGAINST THE NEGATIVE STEREOTYPES OF TECHNICAL PEOPLE THAT ARE OFTEN PORTRAYED IN THE MEDIA.
© 1991 United Feature Syndicate, Inc.
YOU BROKE MY CONCENTRATION.

WELCOME TO THE "SCIENTIST ANTI-DEFAMATION LEAGUE" WEEKLY MEETING.
TONIGHT'S TOPIC IS THE STEREOTYPE THAT WE SCIENTISTS HAVE NO SOCIAL LIVES...
BUT FIRST...
© 1991 United Feature Syndicate, Inc.
IS SATURDAY NIGHT OKAY FOR OUR NEXT MEETING?
I'M FREE
NO PROBLEM
WIDE OPEN

I'D LIKE TO START OUR "SCIENTIST ANTI-DEFAMATION LEAGUE" MEETING WITH A FILM ABOUT STEREOTYPES.
DO WE HAVE A VOLUNTEER TO RUN THE PROJECTOR?
© 1991 United Feature Syndicate, Inc.
ME
ME
ME
ME
ME
ME
ME

AT THE "SCIENTIST ANTI-DEFAMATION LEAGUE" WE MUST DISPEL SOCIETY'S NOTION THAT SCIENTISTS ARE ALWAYS MALE.
UNFORTUNATELY, OUR MEMBERSHIP IS TOTALLY MALE BECAUSE ALL OF YOU JOINED JUST TO MEET WOMEN.
ANY IDEAS?
© 1991 United Feature Syndicate, Inc.
MAYBE WE COULD MERGE WITH THE "AEROBIC INSTRUCTOR ANTI-DEFAMATION LEAGUE."

HONESTY

For humans, honesty is a matter of degree. Engineers are always honest in matters of technology and human relationships. That's why it's a good idea to keep engineers away from customers, romantic interests, and other people who can't handle the truth.

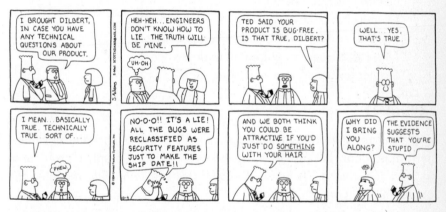

Engineers sometimes bend the truth to avoid work. But thanks to the concept of "common usage" this is not technically dishonest in the modern workplace.

Sometimes engineers say things that sound like lies but technically are not because nobody could be expected to believe them. The complete list of engineer lies is listed below.

"I won't change anything without asking you first."

"I'll return your hard-to-find cable tomorrow."

"I *have* to have new equipment to do my job."

"I'm not jealous of your new computer."

FRUGALITY

Engineers are notoriously frugal. This is not because of cheapness or mean spirit; it is simply because every spending situation is simply a problem in optimization, that is, "How can I escape this situation while retaining the greatest amount of cash?"

ADVICE

Engineers are always delighted to share wisdom, even in areas in which they have no experience whatsoever. Their logic provides them with inherent insight into any field of expertise. This can be a problem when dealing with the illogical people who believe that knowledge can only be derived through experience, as in this case:

EXPLAINING ENGINEERING

Most people don't know what it means to be an engineer. There are many types of engineers and they do many fascinating things during the workday. However, the excitement and pure adrenaline rush of the engineer's life is sometimes lost when it is explained to other people.

POWERS OF CONCENTRATION

If there is one trait that best defines an engineer it is the ability to concentrate on one subject to the complete exclusion of everything else in the environment. This sometimes causes engineers to be pronounced dead prematurely.

There are numerous reports* of engineers who were halfway through the embalming process before they sat up and shouted something like

---

*I can't remember where I saw these reports, but when I think of it I'll mail you copies.

"I've got it—all it needs is a backup relay circuit!!!" Some funeral homes in high-tech areas have started checking résumés before processing the bodies. Anybody with a degree in electrical engineering or experience in computer programming is propped up in the lounge for a few days just to see if he or she snaps out of it.

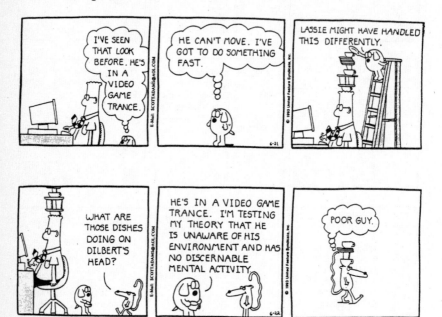

RISK

Engineers hate risk. They try to eliminate it whenever they can. This is understandable, given that when an engineer makes one little mistake the media will treat it like it's a big deal or something.

EXAMPLES OF BAD PRESS FOR ENGINEERS

- *Hindenberg.*

- Space Shuttle *Challenger.*

- Hubble space telescope.

- *Apollo 13.*

- *Titanic.*

- Ford Pinto.

- Corvair.

The risk/reward calculation for engineers looks something like this:

RISK

Public humiliation and the death of thousands of innocent people

REWARD

A certificate of appreciation in a handsome plastic frame

Being practical people, engineers evaluate this balance of risks and rewards and decide that risk is not a good thing. The best way to avoid risk is by advising that any activity is technically impossible for reasons that are far too complicated to explain.

If that approach is not sufficient to halt a project, then the engineer will fall back to a second line of defense:

"It's technically possible but it will cost too much."

The quickest way to make a project uneconomical is by doubling the resources needed and using the cover story that you need to prevent failures.

EGO

Ego-wise, two things are important to engineers:

- How smart they are.

- How many cool devices they own.

The fastest way to get an engineer to solve a problem is to declare that the problem is unsolvable. No engineer can walk away from an unsolvable problem until it's solved. No illness or distraction is sufficient to get the

engineer off the case. These types of challenges quickly become personal—a battle between the engineer and the laws of nature.

Engineers will go without food and hygiene for days to solve a problem.
(Other times just because they forgot.) And when they succeed in solving
the problem they will experience an ego rush that is better than sex—and
I'm including the kind of sex where other people are involved. Not only is
it better at the moment, but it lasts for as long as people will listen to the
engineer's tale of conquest.

Nothing is more threatening to the engineer than the suggestion that
somebody has more technical skill. Normal people sometimes use that
knowledge as a lever to extract more work from the engineer. When an
engineer says that something can't be done (a code phrase that means it's
not fun to do), some clever normal people have learned to glance at the
engineer with a look of compassion and pity and say something along these
lines:

"I'll ask Bob to figure it out. He knows how to solve difficult technical
problems."

At that point it is a good idea for the normal person to not stand
between the engineer and the problem. The engineer will set upon the
problem like a starved Chihuahua on a pork chop.

PARDON ME, SIR, BUT I COULDN'T HELP NOTICING THESE EQUATIONS IN YOUR GARBAGE.
I TOOK THE LIBERTY OF CORRECTING A FEW QUANTUM CALCULATIONS.
GOSH. WHY ARE YOU A GARBAGE MAN?
I THINK THE QUESTION IS "WHY ARE YOU AN ENGINEER?"
© 1989 United Feature Syndicate, Inc.

Engineers can actually hear machines talk to them. The rattle in the car's engine teases softly, "I'll bet you can't find me." The computer hums an approving tune when the engineer writes an especially brilliant piece of computer code. The toaster says "Not yet, not yet, not yet" until the toast pops out. An engineer who is surrounded by machines is never lonely and never judged by appearance. These are friends.

So it should be no surprise that engineers invest much of their ego in what kind of "friends" they have.

LET'S SEE... I'VE GOT MY CELLULAR PHONE, MY PAGER, PALM COMPUTER, PERSONAL ORGANIZER, WIRELESS MODEM...
YEAH, I'D SAY I'M PRETTY MUCH THE ENVY OF ENGINEERS EVERYWHERE... LOOKING GOOD... LOOKING GOOD...
WORDS ESCAPE ME...
HERE, I'LL FIRE UP THE OLD THESAURUS.
© 1992 United Feature Syndicate, Inc.

WALLY, I NOTICE THAT ALL YOU HAVE IS A PAGER AND A CALCULATOR WATCH.
UH-OH
THAT'S PATHETIC COMPARED TO MY VAST ARRAY OF PERSONAL ELECTRONICS. DO YOU YIELD TO MY TECHNICAL SUPERIORITY?
WHEN A MALE ENGINEER CHALLENGES ANOTHER FOR DOMINANCE OF THE PACK, THERE IS A BRIEF RITUALISTIC BATTLE RARELY SEEN BY OUTSIDERS.
STAY BACK, I'VE GOT A COMPASS!!
WIRELESS FAX!
AAGH!
© 1992 United Feature Syndicate, Inc.

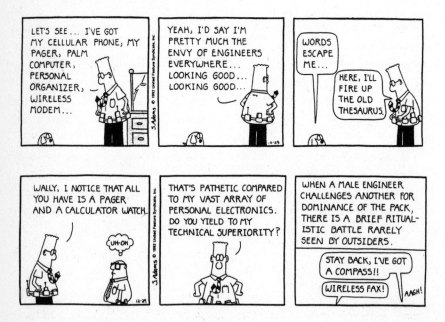

ENGINEERS ILLUSTRATED

I WISH YOU'D REALIZE THAT YOU'RE A GARBAGE MAN, NOT AN ENGINEER. I DON'T NEED YOUR SUGGESTIONS ON MY DESIGNS.
E-Mail: SCOTTADAMS@AOL.COM
WHAT ARE YOU WRITING? OH YEAH, AS IF I CARE.
IF YOU NEED HELP UNDERSTANDING THAT, THE PAPER BOY WILL BE BY SOON. I'VE BEEN WORKING WITH HIM.
© 1993 United Feature Syndicate, Inc.

WHAT HAPPENED WITH THE ROBOT YOU WERE BUILDING?
NOBODY CAN MAKE A ROBOT. IT'S IMPOSSIBLE.
HMM... A PERFECTLY GOOD ROBOT. PROBABLY JUST NEEDS A NEURO-SPECTRUM FIELD CALIBRATION.
THAT WHOLE ROBOT PROJECT WAS BAD FOR MY EGO AS AN ENGINEER.
HEY! GUESS WHO'S WAY SMARTER THAN YOU!
© 1992 United Feature Syndicate, Inc.

DILBERT, YOUR NEW CO-WORKER IS ZIMBU THE MONKEY.
ZIMBU LEARNED ENGLISH FROM THE ZOO KEEPERS IN A SPECIAL PROGRAM.
THIS MONKEY IS AN INSULT TO THE INTELLIGENCE OF THE OTHER WORKERS AND I!
OTHER WORKERS AND "ME," NOT "I."
© 1991 United Feature Syndicate, Inc.

LOOK, ZIMBU, YOU MIGHT HAVE LEARNED LANGUAGE SKILLS AT THE ZOO, BUT IT TAKES MORE THAN THAT TO BE AN ENGINEER.
DILBERT, ZIMBU, LET'S HIT THE CAFETERIA FOR MORNING DONUTS.
OKAY, AFTER TEN A.M. IT TAKES MORE THAN LANGUAGE SKILLS TO BE AN ENGINEER.
NOT TODAY-- WE HAVE A STAFF MEET-ING.
© 1991 United Feature Syndicate, Inc.

IT'S TIME TO END THIS CHARADE, ZIMBU!
YOUR LANGUAGE SKILLS ARE SIMPLE ROTE BEHAVIOR. MONKEYS ARE INCAPABLE OF LOGIC AND REASONING.
HA! AND THAT PROGRAM YOU'RE WRITING --IT'S PROBABLY IN "BASIC."
DO YOU EVER WORK?
S. Adams
12-4
© 1991 United Feature Syndicate, Inc.

HEY! DILBERT! IS THAT YOUR NERDMOBILE? HA HA HA!!
E-Mail: SCOTTADAMS@AOL.COM
S. Adams
IT'S MY OLD HIGH SCHOOL NEMESIS, CHUCK.
MAYBE YOU'D LIKE TO RACE ME IN MY CORVETTE. HA HA!
ACTUALLY, CHUCK, IF YOU HAD TAKEN A SCIENCE CLASS YOU'D KNOW THIS IS A "SEEBECK EFFECT" POWER PLANT CAPABLE OF 600 MILES PER HOUR.
ANY IDIOT KNOWS YOU CAN GET MASSIVE POWER SIMPLY BY USING THE SUN TO HEAT THE JUNCTION OF TWO DISSIMILAR WIRES JOINED AT BOTH ENDS.
APPARENTLY I'M FASTER AND SMARTER THAN YOU. AND THESE TAX FORMS SHOW THAT I ALSO EARN MORE THAN YOU.
© 1993 United Feature Syndicate, Inc.
HERE'S A PICTURE OF MY NEW GIRLFRIEND. SHE TEACHES AEROBICS.
10-10
HE'S WINNING. HELP ME OUT HERE, DOGBERT.
STEP ASIDE.
I NOTICE THAT YOUR GIRLFRIEND HAS UNUSUALLY LARGE HANDS AND A VERY PRONOUNCED ADAM'S APPLE.
SO?

THIS IS JUST GREAT... WE ENGINEERS HAVE OLD IBM 286 PCs AND YOU HAVE A SPARC WORKSTATION.
S. Adams E-Mail: SCOTTADAMS@AOL.COM
CORRECT ME IF I'M WRONG, BUT THE ONLY THING YOU KNOW HOW TO DO IS STARE AT THE SCREEN SAVER.
11-18 © 1994 United Feature Syndicate, Inc.
HOW DOES THAT BALL KEEP BOUNCING?
IF ANYBODY NEEDS ME I'LL BE SCROLLING SOME TEXT.

15

CHANGE

"Change" was a very ordinary thing for many eons. But thanks to consultants, "change" has been elevated to an important business concept. It all started with downsizing.

Many managers lost their jobs because of downsizing. These ex-managers wisely called themselves "consultants," because that sounded far sexier than "street urchins."

As the consultants applied their skills, the phrase they used most often was "Spare change?" It began as a plaintive mumble, but over time the consultants became more aggressive, shouting *"Spare change!"* to passersby, almost as if it were a command. Over time the phrase was shortened to "change" and it developed into a thriving consulting practice. (I might have some of the details wrong, but I know the story involves consultants asking for money.)

The best thing about change consulting is that it can be sold to just about any company. Businesses are experiencing more changes than a bunch of babies in a beer-drinking contest.*

The consultant's sales pitch works like this:

Consultant: "So, are you planning to change anything?"

Manager: "Well . . . yeah, I suppose."

Consultant: "Do you have a change management plan in place?"

Manager: "What's that?"

Consultant: *"You're doomed!!!* Give me money, quick!"

---

*Yes, this analogy is uncalled for and it adds no value to the chapter. But I worked all morning on it and I'm not willing to throw it out.

FEAR OF CHANGE

People hate change, and with good reason. Change makes us stupider, relatively speaking. Change adds new information to the universe; information that we don't know. Our knowledge—as a percentage of all the things that can be known—goes down a tick every time something changes.

And frankly, if we're talking about a percentage of the total knowledge in the universe, most of us aren't that many basis points superior to our furniture to begin with. I hate to wake up in the morning only to find that the intellectual gap between me and my credenza has narrowed. That's no way to start the day.

On the other hand, change is good for the people who are causing the change. They understand the new information that is being added to the universe. They grow smarter in comparison to the rest of us. This is reason enough to sabotage their efforts. I recommend sarcasm with a faint suggestion of threat.

Changer: "I hope I can count on your support."

You: "No problem. I'll be delighted to jeopardize my short-term goals to help you accomplish your career objectives."

Changer: "That's not exactly—"

You: "I don't mind feeling like a confused rodent and working long hours, especially if the payoff is a new system that I vigorously argued against."

The goal of change management is to dupe slow-witted employees into thinking change is good for them by appealing to their sense of adventure and love of challenge. This is like convincing a trout to leap out of a stream to experience the adventure of getting deboned. (Trout are not team players.)

To overcome the natural reluctance of the victims, consultants have developed a battery of advanced management techniques that I have summarized below for your convenience.

CONTENT-FREE COMMUNICATIONS

Faced with change, employees have one question: "What's going to happen to me?" A successful change management communication program will avoid that question.

Rarely does a business change result in everybody being happy and nobody getting the shaft. That can be a problem because change requires the participation of all parties, including the eventual shaftees. For management, the trick is to string everybody along until the change is complete and the losers can be weeded out for shaftage.

Communication about change is a lot like a wooden hamburger. (Work with me here.) If you put enough garnish on it, somebody is going to swallow it. Not coincidentally, the same people who might eat a wooden hamburger (let's call them the "ungifted" people) are the ones singled out for victimization after a major change.

You can fool the ungifted wood-eaters by having plenty of meetings, e-mail messages, newsletters, and voice mail broadcasts that speak of good things ahead without addressing specific people. The eventual victims will start to believe they are part of the golden future. With luck, they might even be duped into becoming "Change Masters."

CHANGE MASTERS

Employees are told that if they embrace change they will be hailed as "Change Masters" instead of hapless victims. This is the adult equivalent of being a Mighty Morphin Power Ranger except without the cool outfits and action figures. Given the choice of being a Change Master or not, I'd certainly want to be one, just on the off chance it would give me X-ray vision.

The cynical employees who prefer to stay uninvolved while baiting the Change Masters have a name too. They are called the "Change Master Baiters." But that's another book.

PERPETUAL MOTION

Change is caused by consultants. Then you need consultants to tell you how to handle the change. When you're done changing you need consultants to tell you that the environment has changed and you'd better change again.

It's a neat little perpetual motion machine. That's the problem when you pay consultants by the hour. In some small towns there is a rule that consultants can't serve as volunteer firemen. The fear is that they'd drive around setting fire to the town.

16

BUDGETING

The budget process was invented by an alien race of sadistic beings who resemble large cats. The cat aliens taught budgeting to the Egyptian pharaohs, who used it as punishment during the construction of the pyramids. That explains how twenty-ton slabs of rock were carried for miles by as few as three people.

The diabolical plan of the cat aliens was to torment large segments of the human population at once, then come back later and chow down. Tragically, the cat people parked their mother ship in a warm spot of the galaxy, curled up to take naps, and ended up getting sucked into the sun.

Over the years the true purpose of the budget process was lost. Now, due to an unfortunate misinterpretation* of hieroglyphics, budgeting is seen as a method of controlling spending at big companies. Ironically, this goal has been accomplished primarily by removing managers from the productive flow—where they would otherwise be tempted to spend money—and trapping them in meetings that can last for months.

Contrary to what you might expect from the word "budget," it is not a fixed amount. It will change many times throughout the year to take advantage of the principle of "Budget Uncertainty":

*The hieroglyphic for "meeting" is very similar to the symbol for "*Ouch!!* A sphinx sat on my leg!"

If you change the budget often enough, the employees will begin acting like gophers on a rifle range, afraid to do anything that draws attention. And where there is fear there is low spending. And where there is low spending there are huge stock options for senior management, followed by an eventual death spiral of the corporation.

I had a point when I started all that, but I suspect it was not a compelling one.

PADDING YOUR BUDGET

You can guarantee that you get your fair share of the budget pie by exaggerating your value and your requirements. While it's true that every single manager has used this technique since the first caveman requested two burnt sticks to scratch on the cave wall, it can still work for you.

Your boss will expect you to come in with a high number that will then be whittled down in the time-honored battle between the clueless and the dishonest.

Some employees make the naive mistake of asking for twice as much as they need. The boss will see right through that clumsy maneuver and cut the request in half. (Bosses aren't as dumb as they look!)

The solution—which seems obvious to me—is to ask for several billion dollars more than you need. If, for example, you need three personal computers for your department, you could ask for $50 billion. This will be met with angry stares, sometimes even profanity. But if you only end up with, say, twenty percent of what you requested, that's still a cool $10 billion. And that means an end to "out of memory" error messages forever.

DEFENDING YOUR BUDGET

Management will try to trim the budget by sending an army of low-ranking, clueless budget analysts to interview you and ask insightful questions such as: "What could you do if you had half the budget you have now?"

Your first impulse might be to toss your head back and laugh in that mocking, self-righteous tone that you reserve for the "special" clueless.

Don't follow that impulse.

It's best to humor budget analysts. They make recommendations to management about budget cuts. Pretend to be interested in them personally (as if you would have a friend who spends all day doing budget work). People who work in budget departments do not have any real friends so they have no frame of reference to determine if you're just yanking their chains. Sometimes you can protect millions of dollars in your budget simply by buying a bag of cookies, dropping it on the budget analyst's desk, and saying something deeply personal such as "How was your weekend, big guy?"

When you are forced to defend your budget there are two techniques to keep in mind (1) lying and (2) lying.

You might feel some ethical discomfort about lying. The feeling will go away after the first time you tell the truth and discover that your budget

has been cleaned out like the last bag of potato chips at a Grateful Dead*
concert. In the worst case, you'll get used to lying. Eventually, you'll
develop a strong preference for it.

Lying does not come easily to some people. Study these examples to get
a better feel for the technique:

Wrong

"Well, since ninety percent of everything we do is a failure, and nobody on
the team thinks a customer would buy the product anyway, I'd say you
could put my whole department in a burlap bag, drown us in the river, and
come out ahead of the game."

Correct

"Good Lord, man!!! Are you Satan's spawn?? Don't you realize that if you
cut even one dollar from our budget it will set off a chain reaction that
could alter the rotation of the planet, melt the polar ice caps, and con-
demn us all to a frosty death!!!??"

Wrong

"Okay, you caught me. We don't need all of this money. It was just a ploy
to puff up my personal empire and get me promoted so I can have an
attractive executive assistant to take with me on trips."

Correct

"Aaaagh!!!! How can you even think such a thing! I'm operating on a shoe-
string. I'm chipping in my own money. But that's okay, because I believe in
this project, unlike the bloated, overfunded 'Project Unicorn' down the
hall. And if you talk to them, tell them I said you do not look like a Mister
Potato Head."

---

*This analogy was written prior to the untimely demise of Jerry Garcia. But I like it so much I
decided to keep it as a reminder of the importance of preserving our rain forests.

Always provide confusing charts and spreadsheets to support your budget requests. There's no such thing as too much information when it comes to defending your budget. Boredom and confusion are your allies in the budget fight.

Your budget charts and spreadsheets should look complicated enough to convey two messages:

1. "I have researched my budget requirements thoroughly."

2. "Smart people would understand this chart. Don't you be one of the 'other' people."

SPEND IT ALL

Whatever you do, don't leave any money in your budget at the end of the year. This is perceived by your management as a sign of failure and weakness, not to mention poor forecasting. Your budget for next year will be decreased accordingly as punishment.

Your management wouldn't give you all that money if it didn't want you to spend it. However, it might be necessary to loosen your definition of what types of expenses are vital to the health of the company. I recommend ordering large cargo containers of paper towels to make up whatever budget underruns you have. Paper products are always useful and they have the advantage of being completely flushable if you need to make room in the storage area later.

BUDGETING ILLUSTRATED

I'M FROM THE FINANCE DEPARTMENT. I'M HERE TO REDUCE COSTS.
S.Adams E-mail: SCOTTADAMS@AOL.COM
IT MIGHT SEEM LIKE ALL I DO IS COME UP WITH SHORT-SIGHTED WAYS TO SAVE MONEY WHILE MAKING YOUR JOB HARDER. BUT THERE'S ANOTHER SIDE TO THIS STORY.
AND THAT WOULD BE...?
I FORGET.
6/20 © 1995 United Feature Syndicate, Inc. (NYC)

I SUMMARIZED THE BUDGET IMPACTS ON SIX HUNDRED PROJECTS WITH THOSE THREE BULLET POINTS.
S.Adams © 1993 United Feature Syndicate, Inc.
" - OXYGEN IS GOOD
- COMPETITION IS BAD
- I LIKE JELLO "
3-16
DO YOU THINK IT'S TOO DETAILED FOR THE SENIOR EXECUTIVES?
TAKE OUT THE "COMPETITION" ONE.
Internet: scottAdams@AOL.com

I FOUND A TYPO IN THE BUDGET SPREAD-SHEET... IT'S TOO LATE TO FIX IT.
S.Adams © 1993 United Feature Syndicate, Inc.
WE TRANSFERRED ONE JOB TO ANOTHER GROUP BUT ACCIDENTALLY KEPT THE MONEY AND HEAD-COUNT.
2-17
... SO, WE STILL PAY YOU BUT YOU AREN'T ALLOWED TO DO WORK.
THIS IS THE HAPPIEST DAY OF MY LIFE.
Internet: scottAdams@AOL.com

BOOM!
S.Adams E-Mail: SCOTTADAMS@AOL.COM
CRASH!
1-8-94
I HEAR YOUR COMPANY IS TRIMMING TRAVEL BUDGETS.
CAN ANYONE LEND ME BUS FARE TO GET HOME?
© 1993 United Feature Syndicate, Inc.

THE COMPANY IS A BILLION DOLLARS BELOW ITS EARNINGS PROJECTIONS.
FROM NOW ON, ONLY THE MANAGERS AT MY LEVEL OR ABOVE MAY EAT DONUTS AT COMPANY MEETINGS.
THIS WON'T BE EASY FOR ANY OF US. HECK, I DON'T EVEN KNOW IF I CAN EAT THIS MANY DONUTS.

I DECIDED TO CUT YOUR PROJECT FUNDING IN HALF BUT KEEP THE OBJECTIVES THE SAME.
IT'S A BRILLIANT PLAN. WE GET ALL THE BENEFITS AT HALF THE COSTS!
WHY IS IT THAT THE NUTTIEST PEOPLE DEFINE REALI-TY?
AND WHY COULDN'T I REWRITE THE BUSINESS CASE TO INCREASE REVE-NUE?

DILBERT, GO DOWN TO THE ACCOUNTING DEPARTMENT AND FIND OUT WHAT THESE FIGURES MEAN.
GULP
NO... P-PLEASE... THEY AREN'T EVEN HUMAN THERE !!!
I DON'T LIKE HIM.
SURPRISE.

THIS MUST BE THE COMPANY ACCOUNTING DEPARTMENT.
I... I NEED TO ASK SOME QUESTIONS ABOUT THIS B-BUDGET REPORT.
IS THIS A BAD TIME FOR YOU?
ALWAYS.

FOOL! WHY HAVE YOU COME TO THE ACCOUNTING DEPARTMENT?!!
UH... I HAD SOME QUESTIONS, SIR... MA'AM ... ER, SIR?
ARE YOU A MAN OR WOMAN?
IN ACCOUNTING, IT DOESN'T REALLY MATTER.
© 1990 United Feature Syndicate, Inc.
S. Adams
8-15

SO... YOU'VE COME TO THE ACCOUNTING DEPARTMENT FOR AN EXPLANATION OF THE BUDGET REPORT, AYE?
UNCHAIN HIM, BRADLEY.
NORMALLY WE WOULD TORTURE AND KILL YOU FOR QUESTIONING OUR REPORT.
BUT YOU REALIZED THAT MY QUESTIONS ARE VALID?
NO. I'M PROMOTING BRADLEY. YOU'RE MY NEW ANALYST.
© 1990 United Feature Syndicate, Inc.
8-16
S. Adams

NO! YOU CAN'T FORCE ME TO WORK IN ACCOUNTING! I'M AN ENGINEER!
IT'S TOO LATE...
YOU CAME... YOU BREATHED THE AIR ... THE CHANGE IS IRREVERSIBLE ... BRADLEY WILL TRAIN YOU.
I'M STARTING TO GET A BAD ATTITUDE ABOUT THIS JOB...
GOOD. I CAN SKIP THAT PART OF THE TRAINING.
© 1990 United Feature Syndicate, Inc.
S. Adams
8-17

DILBERT IS FORCED TO WORK IN THE ACCOUNTING DEPARTMENT
FIRST YOU MUST UNDERSTAND HOW NUMBERS CHANGE REALITY...
Numbers Change
S. Adams
SOME PEOPLE THINK NUMBERS MERELY REFLECT REALITY... BUT WE BELIEVE THAT NUMBERS CREATE REALITY.
Numbers Change Reality!
8-18
THIS IS OUR BUDGET-ERASING ROOM...
ERASE FASTER!!
SNAP
© 1990 United Feature Syndicate, Inc.

TRUE TALES OF ACCOUNTING

From: (name withheld)
To: scottadams@aol.com

Scott,

A few years ago the local management turned off the down escalators to save some money, no kidding. This was soon ended after the manager who was responsible gave a presentation to the visiting CEO, using this as an example of how creative he was in saving money.

From: (name withheld)
To: scottadams@aol.com

Scott,

Our company solicited ideas for cost cutting. Someone decided that we could save "X" amount of dollars by eliminating feminine hygiene products in the women's bathrooms. Our new gung-ho personnel director decided this was really neat, and announced the new proclamation to the whole company via e-mail.

Needless to say, the women in the company flamed this guy to a well-done crisp. The amount of estimated savings was close to the total amount that we pay the janitorial service, which provides these products for no extra cost.

The e-mail got hotter: "The idea is sexist," "We should get rid of the coffee machines," "Eliminate executive bonuses . . ."

What finally shut everyone up and got the procedure reversed was e-mail from a manager who told about a female sales exec he knows. When she is involved in a deal with a prospective client, she always checks the feminine hygiene supplies in that company's bathrooms. If the supplies are missing, she knows the company is going down the tube.

RELATED STORY OF MY OWN

A Pacific Bell co-worker of mine determined that the janitor service was removing the used rolls of toilet paper from the stalls well before the final square was used. To him, this was a huge waste and maybe even some sort of elaborate janitorial scam.

I talked him out of the conspiracy theory, but he was convinced that action was needed. He spent the afternoon crafting an elaborate memo on this problem, complete with calculations of costs, and sent it to the Facilities Department for action.

He's still waiting for a reply.

SALES

If your company's products are overpriced and defective you can compensate by having a good sales incentive plan. No problem is so great that it cannot be overcome by a salesperson who has the proper motivation.

For example, it is well-documented that a frightened ninety-pound woman can generate enough adrenaline to lift a Chrysler minivan that has parked on her foot. Experiments have also shown that after the third time you park the minivan on her foot she will slay the researchers with a mechanical pencil and scream something like "DON'T EVER ASK ME TO BE A TEMPORARY SECRETARY AT THIS HELLHOLE AGAIN!!!" The strange thing about it is that the woman will scream in all capital letters. And that's my point: People can do almost anything if they have the proper incentive.

If sales at your company are low, it's because the sales force does not have the proper incentives. This situation is easily remedied. All you have to do is raise the sales quotas until the sales force must choose between two lifestyles:

A. A life of deception and treachery.

B. A life in a trailer park.

Salespeople can only survive for about three minutes in a trailer park. That's how long it takes the other residents to hunt them down and kill them. (Trailer park residents tend to have bitter memories of the salespeople who convinced them that metal is a good material for keeping summer heat out.)

Smart salespeople will choose option number one—a life of deception and treachery. That's something they can get used to, and with patience and practice, they can learn to enjoy it. There are few pleasures greater than selling defective products to obnoxious customers. It's not something you'd brag about to the grandkids, but it feels better than a good sneeze in the forest.

Selling isn't easy. Sure, anybody can sell high-quality products at reasonable prices. There's no trick to that. The real art of selling comes in when your product sucks compared to the competition. Your company's Marketing Department can only go so far in closing that gap. (See Chapter 11 on marketing.) The sales force must do the rest. Here are some tips for becoming a world-class sales professional:

Avoid Discussing Costs

Never discuss the true cost of your product with customers. It only encourages them to make rational decisions. Focus on the many "intangible" economic benefits your company offers. And remember that confusion is your friend in sales.

Example:

"If you bank with us, your money will accrue tax-free inflation from the first day!"

Irrelevant Comparisons

Prey on the natural stupidity of the average customer. Most people wouldn't know the difference between a logical argument and a porcupine strapped to their forehead.° Steer the customer toward silly and irrelevant comparisons.

Example:

"Well, sure, maybe forty-eight miles per hour isn't an impressive peak speed for a sports car, but you have to compare that to hopping."

Be a "Partner"

Become a "partner" with your customer, not just a vendor. The distinction is important. A vendor simply takes the customer's money and provides a product. A partner takes the customer's money and provides a "solution" that looks suspiciously like a "product" except it costs more.

A partner works with customers to help them define their requirements. This can be a problem if the only thing that makes your product

---

°At last, an analogy that isn't "pointless."

distinctive is its flaws. For example, in the case of the sports car that has a peak speed of forty-eight miles per hour, you can emphasize safety as a major advantage.

Example:

"If you don't count starvation, nobody has ever died in one of these sports cars. That's gotta be your top concern."

Attitude

Optimism is contagious. A professional salesperson will avoid negative phrases and use only positive-sounding words.

DON'T SAY	DO SAY
Old technology	Backward compatible
Overpriced	Premium
Unavailable	Can't keep it on the shelf
Piece of shit	Stands alone
Incompatible	Proprietary

Find the Decision-Makers

A sales professional should always try to find the decision-makers in the organization. The decision-makers have the least knowledge of the situation and are therefore more likely to believe whatever the salesperson says.

One reliable way to know if you have found the decision-maker is to examine the office and furnishings of the person in question. Decision-makers are rarely found in anything that resembles a large cardboard box, that is, a "cubicle." And you will never see any of the signs shown below on the wall of an important decision-maker:

"What part of NO didn't you understand?"
"On time. No defects. Pick one."
"Cubicle Sweet Cubicle."

But don't be fooled by an impressive office with a door. Non-decision-makers have offices too. You can test a person's importance in the organization by asking how much RAM his computer has. Anybody who knows the answer to that question is not a decision-maker.

Salespeople can set up meetings with executives of client companies anytime. Employees can't do that. The only way the average employee can speak to an executive is by taking a second job as a golf caddie. Executives hate talking to employees because they always bring up a bunch of unsolvable "issues." Salespeople just buy the executives lunch. It's no contest.

A salesperson can use this access to the executives as a threat to the low-level, cubicle-dwelling, dumb-sign-hanging "recommenders" of the company. Employees live in fear that the executives will hear something bad about them. And rest assured the executives *will* hear something bad about any employee who recommends buying something other than the salesperson's product.

SALES ILLUSTRATED

SO... DILBERT, WELCOME TO THE SALES DEPARTMENT. I'M TINA, YOUR NEW BOSS.
HI
AS THE NEW GUY, YOU GET THE CUSTOMERS WHO DESPISE OUR PRODUCTS AND WANT TO HURT US PERSONALLY.
I HATE YOU! I HATE YOU!
YOU'LL BE SELLING TO THE SMALL BUSINESS MARKET. HE'S YOUR BEST ACCOUNT.
S.Adams
12-15
© 1992 United Feature Syndicate, Inc.

DILBERT THE SALESMAN...
YOUR COMPETITOR WAS HERE AN HOUR AGO...
HE PROMISED ME A MASSAGE FROM HELGA IF I BUY FROM HIS COMPANY. WHAT'S YOUR OFFER?
I'LL GIVE YOU MY HOUSE FOR HELGA.
YOU'RE NEW AT THIS...
S.Adams
12-17
© 1992 United Feature Syndicate, Inc.

AND OUR PRODUCT HAS A THIRTY TERABIT RAM CACHE, JUST LIKE YOUR COMPANY NEEDS. TELL HIM, DILBERT.
IT HAS NO RAM.
AND IT'S CAPABLE OF DETECTING TACHION FIELD EMISSIONS.
YOU'RE CONFUSING US WITH "STAR TREK" AGAIN, STAN.
WE'LL BUILD THAT STUFF INTO THE NEXT FREE UPGRADE.
WE'LL TAKE IT!
BEAM ME UP, SPOCK. THERE'S NO LIFE ON THIS PLANET.
S. Adams E-Mail: SCOTTADAMS@AOL.COM
12-13
© 1993 United Feature Syndicate, Inc.

STAN, YOU PROMISED THE CUSTOMER THINGS THAT ENGINEERING CAN'T POSSIBLY DELIVER. DO YOU KNOW WHAT THIS MEANS?!
IT MEANS I'M A GREAT SALESMAN AND YOU'RE A PUTRID ENGINEER.
MAYBE YOU SHOULD CONSIDER TAKING CLASSES AT NIGHT.
KARATE CLASSES
S. Adams E-Mail: SCOTTADAMS@AOL.COM
12-14
© 1993 United Feature Syndicate, Inc.

I PREDICT SALES TO BE NOTHING FOR TWO YEARS AND THEN TAKE A SUDDEN SURGE.
WHY?
SALES
S. ADAMS
E-Mail: SCOTTADAMS@AOL.COM
THE SURGE WAS ADDED SO I COULD GET THE BUSINESS CASE APPROVED. THE TWO-YEAR LAG GIVES ME TIME TO GET PROMOTED.
SALES
10-10
© 1994 United Feature Syndicate, Inc.
WHAT ABOUT ACCOUNT-ABILITY?
THAT'S WHERE YOU COME IN.

18

MEETINGS

If you're new to the business world, you might mistakenly think that meetings are a boring, sadistic hell, populated by galactic-level morons. I had that same misperception when I joined the working world. Now I understand that meetings are a type of performance art, with each actor taking on one of these challenging roles:

- Master of the Obvious

- Well-Intentioned Sadist

- Whining Martyr

- Rambling Man

- Sleeper

Once you understand the true nature of meetings you can begin to hone your acting skill and create your own character. In this chapter I will describe some of the classic roles, but feel free to combine characters and come up with your own interpretations.

MASTER OF THE OBVIOUS

The Master of the Obvious believes that while he was studying the writings of Plato, Sir Isaac Newton, and Peter Drucker, the rest of the planet was watching "Three's Company" and eating Oreos. The "Master" feels a responsibility to share his wisdom at every opportunity. He knows that any concept—no matter how mundane it might seem to him—will be a cosmic revelation to the raisin-brains around him.

The favored lines of the Master of the Obvious (delivered with great conviction) include:

- "You need customers in order to have revenue!"

- "*Profit* is the difference between *Income* and *Expense*."

- "Training is essential."

- "There is competition in the industry."

- "It's important to retain your good employees."

- "We want a win-win solution."

The secret to being a convincing Master of the Obvious is to combine condescension with sincerity. Your audience must believe that you genuinely wonder how other people can manage to dress themselves and make it to work every day on the first try. And it must seem as though you care.

You can practice for this role while you're alone. All you need is a common table lamp. Lean toward the lamp and repeatedly explain why "electricity is essential" to the illumination process. Continue to restate the thought in different ways. Try to develop a stammer or at least an annoying habit of pausing to think of the right word. Keep practicing until you can make a bulb burn out just by talking to it.

WELL-INTENTIONED SADIST

The Well-Intentioned Sadist believes that meetings should hurt. This is essentially the same attitude taken by the more successful serial killers. In fact, they have the same motto:

"Does this hurt? How about now?"

The Well-Intentioned Sadist has several tools at his disposal for causing discomfort in others. These techniques may be used alone or in any combination:

- Schedule excessively long meetings regardless of the topic.

- Have no clear purpose.

- Have no bathroom breaks (best when combined with coffee).

- Schedule meetings for Friday afternoons or lunchtimes.

This role must be played with a combination of sincerity, dedication, and, most of all, a sociopathic disregard for the lives of other people. You can get in the right mood by continually watching movies in which the star's family gets massacred and later his dog dies while taking a bullet for him. (Look for titles that feature exceptionally bad actors who are good at martial arts.)

WHINING MARTYR

Whining Martyrs get a lot of stage time. That's why there is so much competition for the role. People will detest you for being a Whining Martyr, but that can fuel your creative fires. With performance art, the audience is part of the show.

As a Whining Martyr, you should craft your complaints into tales that illustrate how valuable and intelligent you are compared to the obstructionist dolts who surround you. Imagine that your co-workers are trying to stymie your every move, now add a dash of self-pity, and voilà—you have the perfect Whining Martyr attitude.

Recommended Whines

"It looks like I'll have to sit in for the boss *again.*"

"Don't worry about taking the last of the coffee. I'll just use my pen to scrape some of the residue off the inside of the pot and chew on it during the meeting."

"I can't believe the CEO wants *another* meeting with me."

"[Sigh] . . . Yes, I can do that for you . . . I'll have time on Saturday night, as usual. It's no problem, since my spouse left me and took the kids."

"Boy, I'd *love* to be able to take sick days like you people who don't have work to do."

"*Another* meeting? There goes the last lunch break I could have taken this fiscal year."

RAMBLING MAN

Most of the major roles at a meeting can be played by a male or a female. But the part of "Rambling Man" can only be played by a male. Women sometimes try to take on this role, but it always comes across as "babbling"* instead of true "rambling."

The Rambling Man's role is to redirect any topic toward an unrelated event in which he participated. The unrelated event might have a humorous climax, but more often than not it's just a way to let everybody know how clever he is.

The Master of the Obvious can be an accomplice to the Rambling Man, occasionally saying things like "It gets cold in Minnesota during the winter." These comments are construed as encouragement to continue and can make the entire scene last for hours.

Rambling Man is usually a cameo role and not a recurring character in regularly scheduled meetings. That's because even the Well-Intentioned Sadist and the Whining Martyr tire of this character. (And they *enjoy* pain.)

The Rambling Man clicks best when combined with the Sleeper, described below.

---

*Unlike rambling, babbling is related to the topic, yet somehow it lasts a long time without conveying any useful information. Men and women can both babble, but only men are successful ramblers.

SLEEPER

The Sleeper is essentially a stage prop. There are no lines involved in this role. You are expected to dress fashionably, but not so flamboyantly that you detract attention from the actors who have speaking parts.

It is acceptable to nod the head gently when the other actors are speaking. This suggests the gentle swaying of a tree in the wind. You may also eat pastries and drink coffee. If trapped into responding verbally, as a last resort you can use one of these phrases:

- "Uh huh."

- "Nothing new to report."

- "Same ol' same ol'"

- "You got that right" (said with slight hillbilly accent).

19

PROJECTS

If you're not on a "project," then you probably have a thankless, boring, repetitive job. You're like an ant carrying crumbs back to the ant hole over and over again.

But if you *are* working on a project, life is very different. You're still an ant carrying crumbs, of course, but there's a Russian Squat-Dancing° festival between you and the anthill. And you spend much of your waking hours fantasizing about how great it would be to have a thankless, boring, repetitive job.

°Yeah, I'm sure there's another name for it. But they *should* call it Squat-Dancing.

This chapter is for the benefit of those of you who are considering being on a project.

Executive summary: RUN AWAY!! RUN AWAY!!

There are several distinct stages to every project, regardless of the purpose of the project. I will discuss each of them separately, because if I discussed them all at the same time it would look somewhat random. Can't have that.

NAMING THE PROJECT

The success of any project depends primarily on two things:

1. Luck

2. A great project name

There's nothing you can do about luck, except maybe rub garlic on a penny and keep it in your sock. That's what I do. It's not an ancient tradition or anything like that; I just like the way it makes me feel. And who knows, maybe that's how ancient traditions get started. Somebody has to go first.

If you're doing all you can do in the luck department, the next most important task is picking a winning project name. You want a name that conveys strength and confidence. It must be distinct yet easy to remember.

This is the normal process for selecting a winning project name:

1. The project team brainstorms about names.

2. A "multivote" process is used to narrow the choices.

3. The top choice is presented to senior management for approval.

4. A vice president names the project after his favorite Muppet.

TEAM LEADER

The job of Team Leader is often viewed as a stepping stone to a management position. That's because anybody who is gullible enough to take on extra work without extra pay is assumed to have the "right stuff" for management. Given the negative stigma of the job, it's difficult to find somebody willing to volunteer to be a Team Leader. Management is generally forced to conscript a Team Leader based on these qualifications:

- Candidate must know how to make viewgraphs.

- Candidate must be a carbon-based life form.

The Team Leader is typically a person who has no special talent. This characteristic serves the Team Leader well during long meetings. While all the skilled people are squirming around wishing they were out applying their skills, the Team Leader can sit serenely, content in the knowledge that no personal talent is going to waste.

The word "leader" might be debatable in this context, since the job of a Team Leader involves asking people what they should be doing, then asking them how they're doing, then blaming them for not doing it. But leadership takes many forms, and sometimes just being annoying is exactly what the situation requires.

I'M PROMOTING YOU TO TEAM LEADER.
DO I GET A RAISE?
S. Adams
E-Mail: SCOTTADAMS@AOL.COM
THERE'S NO EXTRA MONEY, JUST EXTRA RESPONSIBILITY. IT'S HOW WE RECOGNIZE OUR BEST PEOPLE.
© 1995 United Feature Syndicate, Inc.
1-21
I THOUGHT ALL THE GOOD PEOPLE LEAVE FOR BETTER COMPANIES.
THAT'S ANOTHER WAY TO RECOGNIZE THEM.

WALLY, WOULD YOU LIKE TO BE ON MY "TTP" PROJECT?
WHAT DOES "TTP" STAND FOR?
S. Adams
E-Mail: SCOTTADAMS@AOL.COM
IT'S SHORT FOR THE TTP PROJECT.
5-18
© 1994 United Feature Syndicate, Inc.
I NAMED IT MYSELF... SO, DO YOU WANT TO JOIN?
I'D RATHER BE YOUR ARCH-NEMESIS.

AS YOU KNOW, I'VE BEEN PROMOTED TO TEAM LEADER.
S. Adams
E-Mail: SCOTTADAMS@AOL.COM
WILL YOU DECIDE RAISES?
NO
DO YOU APPROVE EXPENSES?
NO
DO YOU FIRE PEOPLE?
NO
© 1995 United Feature Syndicate, Inc.
1-23
I'M A LEADER, NOT A MANAGER.
WELL, RUN ALONG AND WE'LL BE RIGHT BEHIND YOU.

AS TEAM LEADER, I THINK I SHOULD GET SOME PERKS SO PEOPLE KNOW MY STATUS.
S. Adams
E-Mail: SCOTTADAMS@AOL.COM
I'LL HAVE YOUR CUBICLE WALLS SPRAYED WITH A SPECIAL THICKENING AGENT. IT MIGHT LOOK THE SAME, BUT TRUST ME, PEOPLE WILL KNOW HOW THICK YOU ARE.
© 1995 United Feature Syndicate, Inc.
1-24
I'M JUST LIKE YOU, WALLY, BUT THICKER.
I'VE NOTICED.

REQUIREMENTS

At some point in the project somebody will start whining about the need to determine the project "requirements." This involves interviewing people who don't know what they want but, curiously, know exactly when they need it. These people are called "end users" or simply "pinheads."

Research has shown that there is nothing on this planet dumber than an "end user." The study below ranks the relative intelligence of some common household items this way:

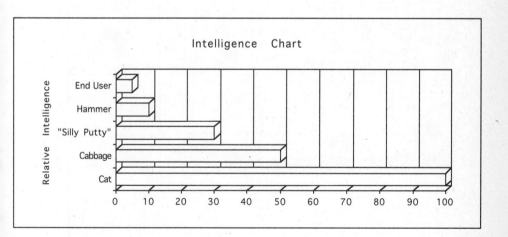

The project team will continue to gather requirements until one of these two conditions is met:

1. The end users forget to breathe, which causes them to die in their sleep.*

2. The project team decides that requirements aren't as important as once thought.

*It's a bigger problem than you'd think.

MANAGEMENT SUPPORT

No project can succeed without management support. The best sort of management support is the kind in which management doesn't find out about the project until it's a market success. If management notices a project too soon it'll support it in the following ways:

- Demand frequent status reports to explain why the team doesn't have enough time to meet deadlines.

- Demand explanations of how the project is different from all the projects that have similar acronyms.

- Ask the team what it could do if it had only half as much funding.

- Appoint an Oversight Committee whose members are always on trips.

To put it another way, managers understand that their role is to remove obstacles from the project team. They could probably do that, with the help of Dr. Kervorkian, but most managers are not such good sports. Therefore, coincidentally, the biggest obstacle to the success of any project is management itself.

SCHEDULING

The scheduling phase of the project involves asking people how long it will take them to do work. It usually goes like this:

Project Leader: "How long will it take to select a vendor?"

Team Member: "Between a day and a year."

Project Leader: "You need to be more specific."

Team Member: "Okay, three years."

Project Leader: "Um, three years is longer than a year."

Team Member: "Fine. You're the expert, *you* pick a time. I quit."

Project Leader: "How about if we say two years?"

Team Member: "Sure, and why don't you pick the vendor while you're at it, since quality obviously means nothing to you."

Eventually this constructive process of give and take will produce an accurate time line for your project. The time line will be transferred onto a complicated chart and hung on the wall of a conference room where it can be conveniently ignored until some external factor determines the actual project due date.

For large projects, Team Leaders use sophisticated project management software to keep track of who's doing what. The software collects the lies and guesses of the project team and organizes them into instantly outdated charts that are too boring to look at closely. This is called "planning."

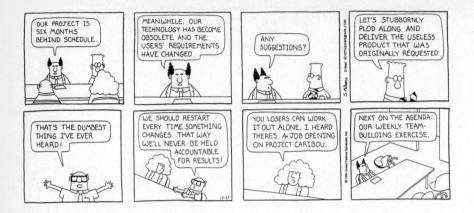

COMPLETING THE PROJECT

PROJECTS ILLUSTRATED

HOW NATURE PROTECTS WEAK PRODUCTS
FIRST, THE ENGINEER PADS HIS SCHEDULE
SIX MONTHS?
AT LEAST.
ONE MONTH TO BUILD THE PRODUCT AND FIVE MONTHS TO PLAY "DOOM" ON MY COMPUTER.
THEN THE MANAGER PADS THE SCHEDULE AS A CLEVER NEGOTIATING PLOY.
ONE YEAR... UNLESS YOU ADD PEOPLE TO MY TINY EMPIRE.
THEN THE VICE PRESIDENT PADS THE SCHEDULE TO AVOID LOOKING BAD TO THE PRESIDENT.
EIGHTEEN MONTHS.
MEANWHILE, THE SALES PEOPLE ARE MAKING UP NUMBERS BECAUSE NOBODY TELLS THEM ANYTHING.
TWO MONTHS... AND IT SOLVES EVERY PROBLEM YOU HAVE!
THIS CAUSES THE CUSTOMERS TO DEVELOP IRRATIONAL DESIRE FOR THE PRODUCT.
GIVE ME THE "BETA" TEST VERSION IN ONE MONTH.
THUS NATURE DISGUISES WEAK PRODUCTS AS "BETA".
CARDBOARD? THAT'S STUPID.
OH... THEN IT'S BETA.

WE JUST HAD A MEET-ING AND DECIDED TO CHANGE YOUR PROJECT SUBSTANTIALLY.
S. Adams E-Mail: SCOTTADAMS@AOL.COM
WE DIDN'T INVITE YOU TO THE MEETING BECAUSE THINGS GO SMOOTHER WHEN NOBODY HAS ANY ACTUAL KNOWLEDGE.
5-21
© 1994 United Feature Syndicate, Inc.
SO, WHAT ARE THE CHANGES?
IF I REMEMBER I'LL LEAVE YOU A VOICE MAIL.

HOW'S YOUR PROJECT COMING ALONG?
S. Adams E-Mail: SCOTTADAMS@AOL.COM
IT'S UNDER-FUNDED AND DOOMED. BUT I'VE GOT SOME GOOD INERTIA GOING AND I'M SETTING UP THE MARKETING DEPARTMENT TO TAKE THE BLAME.
5-20
© 1994 United Feature Syndicate, Inc.
I FEEL LIKE I SHOULD BE DOING SOMETHING HERE.
I'VE GOT YOU SCHEDULED TO MAKE AN UNINFORMED DECISION NEXT WEEK.

HERE'S MY DAILY PROJECT STATUS REPORT.
"MORALE IS LOW. THERE IS TALK OF MUTINY. WE DREAM OF QUITTING AND BECOMING LIFE-GUARDS ON "BAYWATCH." DEATH TO THE POINTY-HAIRED ONE."
HOLY COW! "BAYWATCH" IS HIRING??!
S. Adams E-Mail: SCOTTADAMS@AOL.COM
7-4 © 1994 United Feature Syndicate, Inc.

THE PROBLEM...
WE'RE SO UNDER-STAFFED THAT THE PROJECT IS SIX WEEKS BEHIND SCHEDULE.
THE ANALYSIS...
I CAN'T ADD PEOPLE... I CAN'T CHANGE THE DUE DATE... I CAN'T IGNORE IT.
THE RESULT...
HE WANTS DAILY STATUS REPORTS UNTIL THE SITUATION IMPROVES.
S. Adams E-mail: SCOTTADAMS@AOL.COM
2/17
© 1995 United Feature Syndicate, Inc. (NYC)

I'M CANCELING YOUR PROJECT SO I CAN GIVE YOUR FUNDING TO A PROJECT THAT HAS A MUCH COOLER ACRONYM.
5-25
HA! THE JOKE'S ON YOU! I ANTICIPATED THIS MOVE FROM THE BEGINNING AND HAVE DONE NOTHING BUT CARRY EMPTY BINDERS FOR WEEKS!
BEING GOOD AT YOUR JOB IS LESS FULFILLING THAN YOU MIGHT THINK, DOGBERT.
S. Adams E-Mail: SCOTTADAMS@AOL.COM
© 1994 United Feature Syndicate, Inc.

I'M PUTTING YOU IN CHARGE OF AN IMPORTANT PROJECT WHICH IS FULLY FUNDED.
GASP
I'M A MARKED MAN. THE OTHER EMPLOYEES WILL EITHER TRY TO SUCK UP TO ME FOR MONEY OR THROW BRICKS AT ME.
BUDDY!
THE TRICK IS TO KEEP A PROTECTIVE RING OF SUCK-UPS AROUND AT ALL TIMES.
ZIP!
S. Adams E-Mail: SCOTTADAMS@AOL.COM
5-16
© 1994 United Feature Syndicate, Inc.

I'M ASSIGNING YOU TO "THE PROJECT THAT WOULDN'T DIE."
S. Adams E-Mail: SCOTTADAMS@AOL.COM
EVERYBODY LIKES THIS PROJECT TOO MUCH TO CANCEL IT, BUT NOT ENOUGH TO FUND IT PROPERLY.
AAARG!!
11-14 © 1994 United Feature Syndicate, Inc.
NOW GO OUT THERE AND MAIN-TAIN THE STATUS QUO!
YOU REALLY SHOULDN'T MIX HONESTY WITH YOUR MOTIVATIONAL SPEECHES.

I WANT YOU TO STUDY OUR OPTIONS FOR PROJECT "ZEBRA" AND MAKE A RECOMMENDATION.
S. Adams E-mail: SCOTTADAMS@AOL.COM
TRANSLATION: "READ MY MIND THEN RECOMMEND THE OPTION I'VE ALREADY DECIDED ON."
7/15 © 1995 United Feature Syndicate, Inc. (NYC)
I'LL GET RIGHT ON IT!
TRANSLATION: "I AM DOOMED. I WILL GO LOOK FOR NAUGHTY PICTURES ON THE INTERNET INSTEAD."

I'M PUTTING YOU IN CHARGE OF PROJECT "BIFF."
DILBERT
"BIFF" STANDS FOR "BIG IMPROVEMENTS FOR FREE."
YOUR JOB IS TO RECOMMEND WAYS TO INCREASE PROFITS WITHOUT SPENDING MONEY OR CHANGING ANYTHING.
YOU HAVE TO SPEND MONEY TO MAKE MONEY.
IF WE HAD MONEY TO SPEND WE WOULDN'T NEED TO MAKE MONEY.
DUH
THE POINT IS THAT YOU CAN MAKE MORE MONEY THAN YOU SPEND.
5-28
I'M NOT FOLLOWING YOUR SO-CALLED "POINT."
LOGICALLY, ANYTHING I DON'T UNDERSTAND IS UNIMPORTANT.
HAVE YOUR REPORT TOMORROW.
SO, YOU RECOMMEND... REPLACING ALL MANAGERS WITH LAVA LAMPS.
HERE'S A FEW BUCKS FOR THE LAVA LAMPS.

20

ISO 9000

If your company is not involved in something called "ISO 9000" you probably have no idea what it is. If your company *is* involved in ISO 9000 then you definitely have no idea what it is. Don't ask me what it is; I can't figure it out either. But I have pieced together enough evidence to form a working theory.

My theory: A group of bored Europeans had a few too many Heinekens and decided to play an elaborate prank on the big companies of the world. This prank came to be known as ISO 9000, so named because of the number of beers that were consumed that night. (The phrase "ISO" is either an unintelligible phrase or possibly one of the four hundred European slang words meaning "Is that my beer?")

The inebriated Europeans correctly figured that any silly-ass management technique could become an international craze if they could only keep a straight face when telling people about it. Their "idea" was that if companies documented every process and job description in the organization, this could solve a big problem that businesses have, that is, what to do with all that spare time.

As predicted by the pranksters, customers began hearing about the benefits of ISO 9000 and started demanding that their suppliers get with it. If you aren't ISO 9000 compliant, they reasoned, who knows what you're doing with all that spare time?

Managers at big companies everywhere began documenting everything they did and labeling every tool they used. It was a frenzy of labeling and documenting, labeling and documenting. Slow-moving employees would go home at night and soak in the bathtub to remove the labels slapped on their bodies by overzealous co-workers. It was ugly.

But the effort was not without reward—for consultants. Consultants who were having a tough time selling "Quality" programs quickly reinvented themselves as ISO 9000 experts. To the untrained eye it might seem as though Quality programs and ISO 9000 are not related. I was confused too until one consultant explained it to me this way: "ISO 9000 is closely related to Quality because everything you do is Quality and ISO 9000 documents everything you do, therefore give us money."

I don't think any of us can argue with that.

ISO 9000 ILLUSTRATED

THANK YOU FOR COMING TO THE "ISO 9000" PROJECT KICK-OFF MEETING.
EACH OF YOU WAS HAND-PICKED BY YOUR MANAGER FOR THIS PROJECT BECAUSE...
WELL... NEVER MIND WHY.
S. Adams E-Mail: SCOTTADAMS@AOL.COM
12-7 © 1994 United Feature Syndicate, Inc.

HERE'S THE BASIC PLAN FOR GETTING OUR "ISO 9000" CERTIFICATION.
EACH OF YOU WILL CREATE AN INSANELY BORING, POORLY WRITTEN DOCUMENT. I'LL COMBINE THEM INTO ONE BIG HONKIN' BINDER.
I'LL SEND COPIES TO ALL DEPARTMENT HEADS FOR COMMENT. THEY WILL TREAT IT LIKE A DEAD RACCOON AND ROUTE IT TO THE FIRST PASSERBY.
S. Adams E-Mail: SCOTTADAMS@AOL.COM
12-8 © 1994 United Feature Syndicate, Inc.

WE'RE HAVING AN ISO 9000 AUDIT THIS WEEK.
TAKE A LOOK AT YOUR DOCUMENTED JOB DESCRIPTIONS AND MAKE SURE THAT IT'S WHAT YOU'RE DOING IF THE AUDITOR ASKS.
ACCORDING TO THIS I'M SOME SORT OF ENGINEER.
AS IF WE'D HAVE TIME FOR THAT...
S. Adams E-mail: SCOTTADAMS@AOL.COM
9/25 © 1995 United Feature Syndicate, Inc.(NYC)

I'VE BEEN HIRED BY YOUR COMPANY TO PERFORM AN ISO 9000 AUDIT.
S. Adams E-mail: SCOTTADAMS@AOL.COM
BASICALLY, YOU GIVE ME MONEY AND I TELL YOU THAT YOU'RE A BUNCH OF DOLTS. IT'S THE PERFECT JOB FOR ME.
9/26 © 1995 United Feature Syndicate, Inc.(NYC)
TELL ME WHAT YOU DO HERE, ALICE, IF THAT'S YOUR REAL NAME.
I'M AN ENGINEER. I MAKE SLIDES THAT PEOPLE CAN'T READ. SOMETIMES I EAT DONUTS.

HERE ARE THE RESULTS OF MY ISO 9000 AUDIT OF YOUR COMPANY.
S. Adams E-mail: SCOTTADAMS@AOL.COM
YOUR EMPLOYEES ARE LARGELY UNTRAINED AND - I COULDN'T HELP NOTICE - FAIRLY UNATTRACTIVE.
9/27 © 1995 United Feature Syndicate, Inc.(NYC)
HOWEVER, THEY ARE ALSO HIGHLY SKILLED LIARS, SO YOU PASSED THE AUDIT EASILY.
WE SUCCEED WHERE IT COUNTS !!!

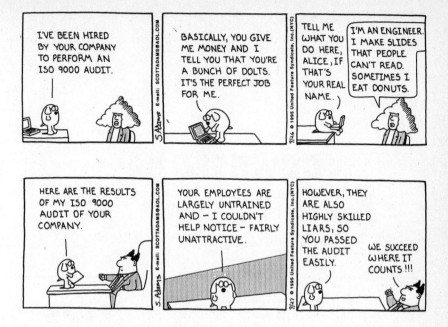

21

DOWNSIZING

When I entered the workforce in 1979 the word "downsize" hadn't been invented yet. A new employee could burrow into the bureaucracy and make a little nest that would last for decades. I felt like a happy little termite living in a Victorian mansion that was always adding another room. I gnawed on the beams, paycheck after paycheck, and nobody ever noticed my tiny teeth marks.

I remember my first "staff" job in a big bank in San Francisco. It was 1980. My partner Dean and I were plucked from the management training program and put on a "special project."

The term "special project" means "All the real jobs are filled by people who, at first glance, don't appear nearly as incompetent as you." That was certainly true in my case. Dean was actually pretty good at appearing competent, but he theorized that he was being punished for something he said to somebody.

Our job was to build a computer information system for the branch banks. We were the perfect people for the job: Dean had seen a computer once, and I had heard Dean talk about it.

Our office was an unused storage room in the basement just off the parking garage, big enough to hold two beat-up desks and some squeaky chairs. It had bare white walls, an uncarpeted floor, no windows, and an annoying echo. It was like a prison cell, but without access to a library and free weights.

Sometimes I would try to call other people in the company to get important information for our project. The response was always the same: "Who are you and why do you want to know?"

I would try to sound important by invoking the first name of the senior vice president and describing how the fate of the free world depended on this vital transfer of information. For example, "Bill needs it . . . to keep our great nation independent."

But somehow they always figured out I was a twenty-two-year-old guy with a bad haircut and a cheap suit sitting in a storage room just off the parking garage. If I was especially charismatic that day, they would have the courtesy to swear at me before hanging up.

Eventually Dean and I degenerated into a pattern of sitting in our little bare room gossiping about co-workers, balancing our checkbooks, and fantasizing about whether the sun was out that day. When we got bored we would hypothesize about the information we needed, talking about it for hours until we were both pretty sure we knew what it "should" be. Then we packaged it up as "user requirements" and gave it to a woman named Barbara who programmed the system in about two weeks. The whole project took about a year, because it's not the type of thing you want to rush.

When it was done, the results of the system were notoriously inaccurate. But our manager assured us that it was okay because he only used the numbers that supported his personal opinion anyway.

It was during this year that I realized the world would run smoothly if companies employed far fewer people like me. In the years that followed, managers all over the world reached the same realization. It was the dawn of downsizing.

The first round of downsizing erased people like Dean and me*—people in jobs that sound good in concept but provide no legitimate value to anybody. The company improved its earnings and nobody worked harder because of it.

The second round of downsizing was tougher. The employees who remained had to work harder to pick up the duties of the departing workers. But in many cases these were "exempt" employees, meaning they would work extra hours without squawking too much about extra pay. Result: The companies improved their earnings. They knew they had a winning strategy here.

For the third round of downsizing, essential jobs were eliminated in huge numbers, but mostly in areas where the impact wouldn't be noticed for at least a year. That includes areas like research, new systems development, business expansion, and training. Result: The companies improved their earnings. There didn't seem to be any bottom to this downsizing well.

The bold companies that are contemplating the fourth round of down-

*Dean and I survived the downsizings by anticipating where they'd happen and slithering into more protected areas.

sizing are relying on the promises of "reengineering" to free up some more human charcoal to fuel the downsizing barbecue. (For a scholarly discussion of reengineering, see Chapter 23.)

The secret to making downsizing work is for managers to recognize the psychological impact. Experiments on laboratory animals show that if you apply continuous electrical shocks to a captive dog, eventually your utility bill will be so high that you'll feel angry at the dog. Companies apply this same medical theory to downsizing. The first rounds of downsizing usually get the people that nobody likes anyway. Those are easy. By the later rounds, managers begin to genuinely hate the remaining employees. They'll become cold-hearted enough to fire family members while humming show tunes. That's when the real savings start.

From E-mail . . .

From: (name withheld)
To: scottadams@aol.com

Scott,

Here's a new one:
You know all about companies trying to get "lean and mean." A friend says her company has now transcended lean and mean. Now it's "skinny and pissed."

MY OWN EXPERIENCES WITH DOWNSIZING

During the banking phase of my career I had the opportunity to work in a variety of jobs for which I was thoroughly unqualified. Fortunately, none of these jobs added value to the company so my incompetence didn't do much damage to the local economy.

At one point I was working as a commercial loan approver for "Professional Loans" (business loans to doctors) even though I had never made a loan or taken a class in lending. Veteran lending officers were instructed to submit their loan proposals to our department for approval. Each loan package was reviewed by all five members of the group (in case anybody missed anything) and then we took it to our boss for the "real" approval.

Although I had no formal training, I learned much on the job:

- Doctors are bad customers because they can prescribe drugs for themselves.

- According to my ex-boss, all Chinese customers cheat on their taxes, thus providing excellent cash flow for repaying loans. (Later I learned this was an unfair generalization.)

- If your co-worker brings his coffee mug to the men's room every day to wash it, you can tell people he goes in there to sit in a stall and drink coffee.

When the downsizing began it didn't hurt much. Instead of five non-value-added people we had four, then three, then eventually only me. I let everybody know that I was "doing the work of five people." I got no sympathy because everybody was "doing the work of five people" if you believed what you heard.

Eventually I left the job. For the past thirteen years, zero people have been doing the work of five people but there were no complaints. This was a fairly clear indication that downsizing had a future.

BRIGHTSIZING

Pessimists point out that the first people to flee a shrinking company are the bright people who can take the "buy-out" packages and immediately get better jobs elsewhere. The dullard employees who remain produce low-quality work, but they compensate by working long hours and producing more low-quality work per person than ever before. The pessimists would have us believe this is a bad thing.

I was one of the people who survived all the early rounds of downsizing, so I know that the pessimists are wrong. Contrary to their gloomy little "logic" I was not producing large volumes of low-quality work after the downsizing. In fact, I moved to a strategy job in which I produced no work whatsoever.

After all the bright people fled, companies realized they had to make downsizing sound like more of a positive development in order to keep morale high.* This was accomplished through a creative process of inventing happier-sounding phrases that all meant essentially the same thing:

"You're fired." (1980)
"You're laid off." (1985)
"You're downsized." (1990)
"You're rightsized." (1992)

*For some reason, morale was low for the employees who realized their workload had tripled, their salaries remained unchanged, and they were still there after all the "good people" had left.

I expect the trend to continue. You'll see the following phrases used within the next five years:

"You're happysized!"
"You're splendidsized!"
"You're orgasmsized!"

From E-mail . . .

From: (name withheld)
To: scottadams@aol.com

Scott,

Here at [company] they have come up with a new way to tell you that you are about to be laid off: It's called "put in the mobility pool."

DOWNSIZING ILLUSTRATED

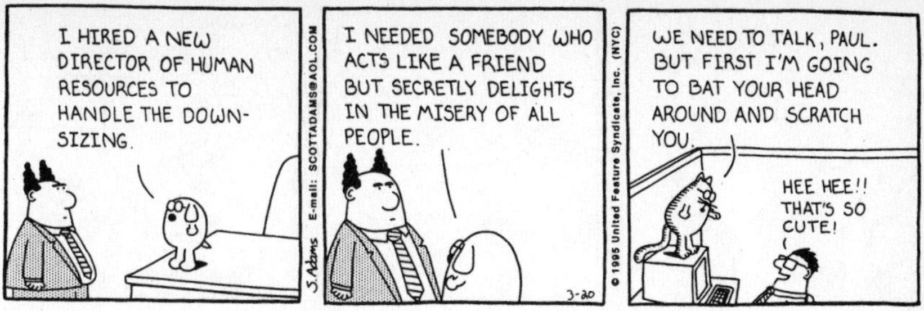
I HIRED A NEW DIRECTOR OF HUMAN RESOURCES TO HANDLE THE DOWN-SIZING.
I NEEDED SOMEBODY WHO ACTS LIKE A FRIEND BUT SECRETLY DELIGHTS IN THE MISERY OF ALL PEOPLE.
WE NEED TO TALK, PAUL. BUT FIRST I'M GOING TO BAT YOUR HEAD AROUND AND SCRATCH YOU.
HEE HEE!! THAT'S SO CUTE!
S. Adams E-mail: SCOTTADAMS@AOL.COM
3-20
© 1995 United Feature Syndicate, Inc. (NYC)

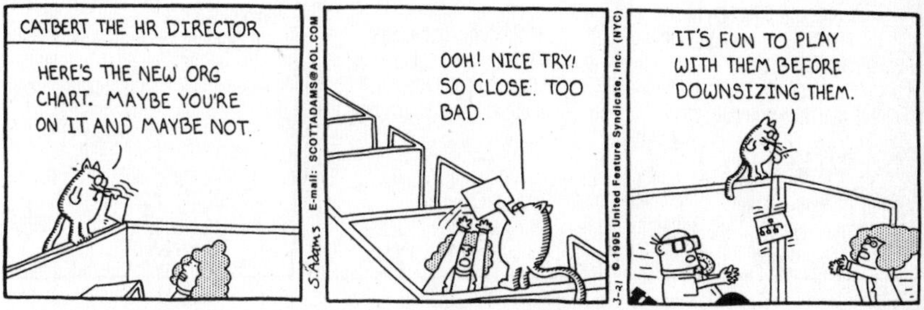
CATBERT THE HR DIRECTOR
HERE'S THE NEW ORG CHART. MAYBE YOU'RE ON IT AND MAYBE NOT.
OOH! NICE TRY! SO CLOSE. TOO BAD.
IT'S FUN TO PLAY WITH THEM BEFORE DOWNSIZING THEM.
S. Adams E-mail: SCOTTADAMS@AOL.COM
3-21 © 1995 United Feature Syndicate, Inc. (NYC)

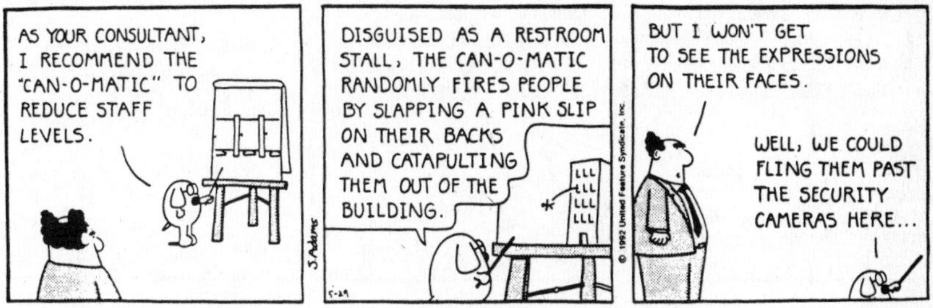
AS YOUR CONSULTANT, I RECOMMEND THE "CAN-O-MATIC" TO REDUCE STAFF LEVELS.
DISGUISED AS A RESTROOM STALL, THE CAN-O-MATIC RANDOMLY FIRES PEOPLE BY SLAPPING A PINK SLIP ON THEIR BACKS AND CATAPULTING THEM OUT OF THE BUILDING.
BUT I WON'T GET TO SEE THE EXPRESSIONS ON THEIR FACES.
WELL, WE COULD FLING THEM PAST THE SECURITY CAMERAS HERE...
S. Adams
© 1992 United Feature Syndicate, Inc.

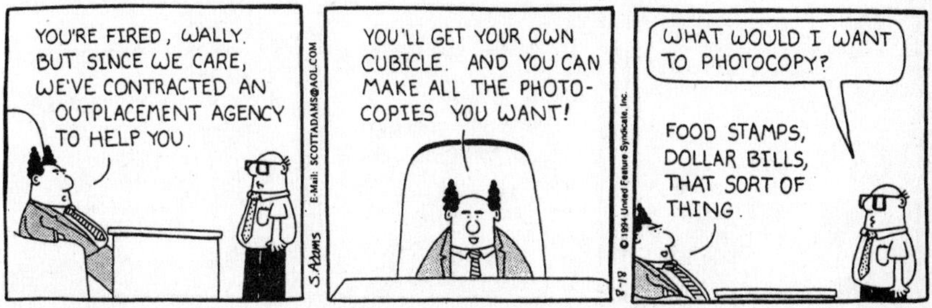
YOU'RE FIRED, WALLY. BUT SINCE WE CARE, WE'VE CONTRACTED AN OUTPLACEMENT AGENCY TO HELP YOU.
YOU'LL GET YOUR OWN CUBICLE. AND YOU CAN MAKE ALL THE PHOTO-COPIES YOU WANT!
WHAT WOULD I WANT TO PHOTOCOPY?
FOOD STAMPS, DOLLAR BILLS, THAT SORT OF THING.
S. Adams E-Mail: SCOTTADAMS@AOL.COM
8-18 © 1994 United Feature Syndicate, Inc.

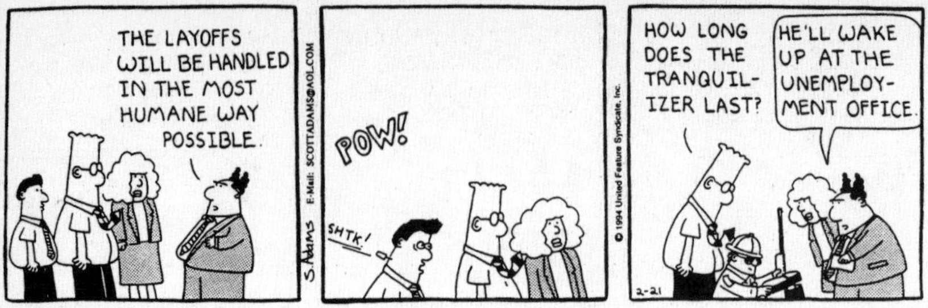
THE LAYOFFS WILL BE HANDLED IN THE MOST HUMANE WAY POSSIBLE.
S. Adams
E-Mail: SCOTTADAMS@AOL.COM
POW!
SHTK!
© 1994 United Feature Syndicate, Inc.
HOW LONG DOES THE TRANQUIL-IZER LAST?
HE'LL WAKE UP AT THE UNEMPLOY-MENT OFFICE.
2-21

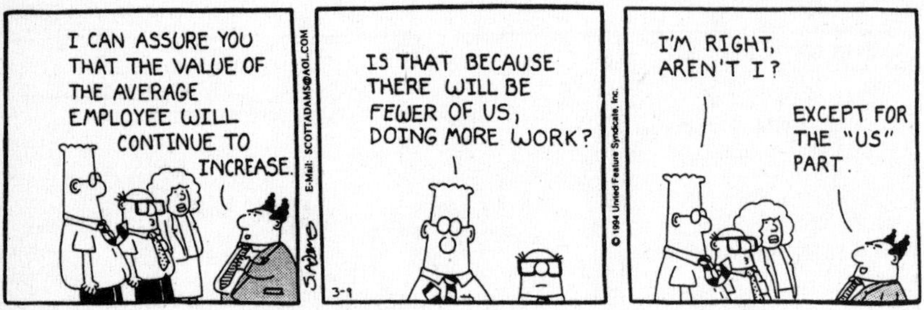
I CAN ASSURE YOU THAT THE VALUE OF THE AVERAGE EMPLOYEE WILL CONTINUE TO INCREASE.
S. Adams
3-9
E-Mail: SCOTTADAMS@AOL.COM
IS THAT BECAUSE THERE WILL BE FEWER OF US, DOING MORE WORK?
© 1994 United Feature Syndicate, Inc.
I'M RIGHT, AREN'T I?
EXCEPT FOR THE "US" PART.

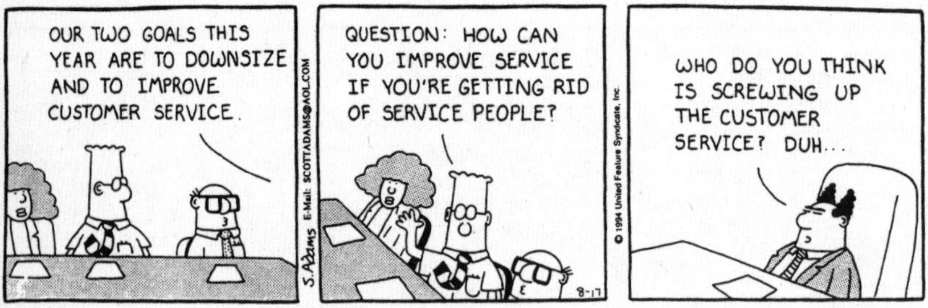
OUR TWO GOALS THIS YEAR ARE TO DOWNSIZE AND TO IMPROVE CUSTOMER SERVICE.
S. Adams
E-Mail: SCOTTADAMS@AOL.COM
QUESTION: HOW CAN YOU IMPROVE SERVICE IF YOU'RE GETTING RID OF SERVICE PEOPLE?
8-17
© 1994 United Feature Syndicate, Inc.
WHO DO YOU THINK IS SCREWING UP THE CUSTOMER SERVICE? DUH...

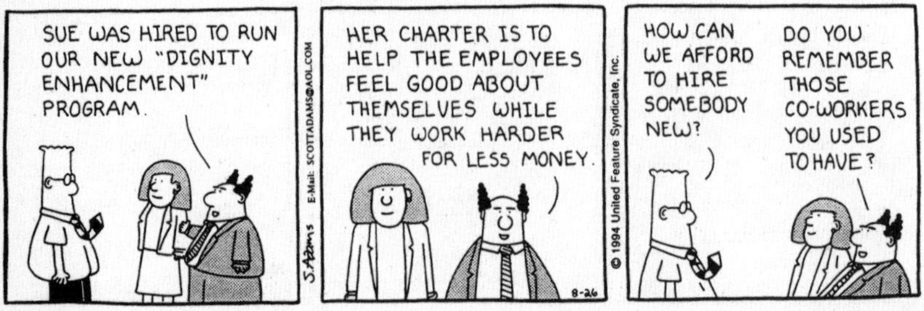
SUE WAS HIRED TO RUN OUR NEW "DIGNITY ENHANCEMENT" PROGRAM.
S. Adams
E-Mail: SCOTTADAMS@AOL.COM
HER CHARTER IS TO HELP THE EMPLOYEES FEEL GOOD ABOUT THEMSELVES WHILE THEY WORK HARDER FOR LESS MONEY.
8-26
© 1994 United Feature Syndicate, Inc.
HOW CAN WE AFFORD TO HIRE SOMEBODY NEW?
DO YOU REMEMBER THOSE CO-WORKERS YOU USED TO HAVE?

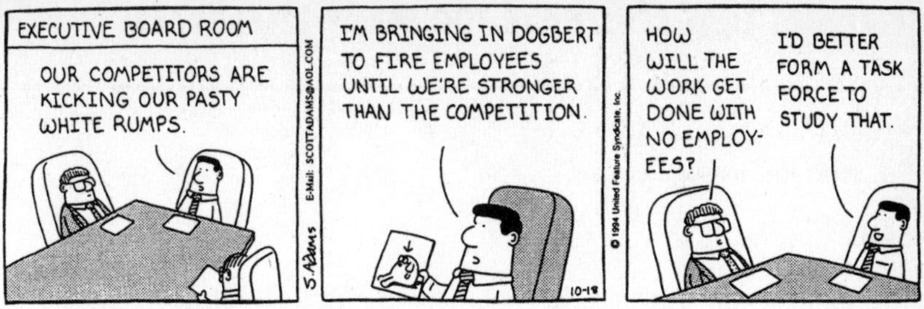
EXECUTIVE BOARD ROOM
OUR COMPETITORS ARE KICKING OUR PASTY WHITE RUMPS.
E-Mail: SCOTTADAMS@AOL.COM
S. Adams
I'M BRINGING IN DOGBERT TO FIRE EMPLOYEES UNTIL WE'RE STRONGER THAN THE COMPETITION.
10-18
© 1994 United Feature Syndicate, Inc.
HOW WILL THE WORK GET DONE WITH NO EMPLOY-EES?
I'D BETTER FORM A TASK FORCE TO STUDY THAT.

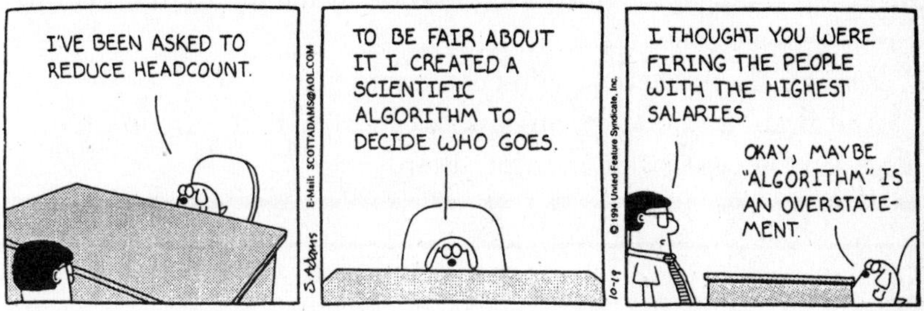
I'VE BEEN ASKED TO REDUCE HEADCOUNT.
E-Mail: SCOTTADAMS@AOL.COM
S. Adams
TO BE FAIR ABOUT IT I CREATED A SCIENTIFIC ALGORITHM TO DECIDE WHO GOES.
10-19
© 1994 United Feature Syndicate, Inc.
I THOUGHT YOU WERE FIRING THE PEOPLE WITH THE HIGHEST SALARIES.
OKAY, MAYBE "ALGORITHM" IS AN OVERSTATE-MENT.

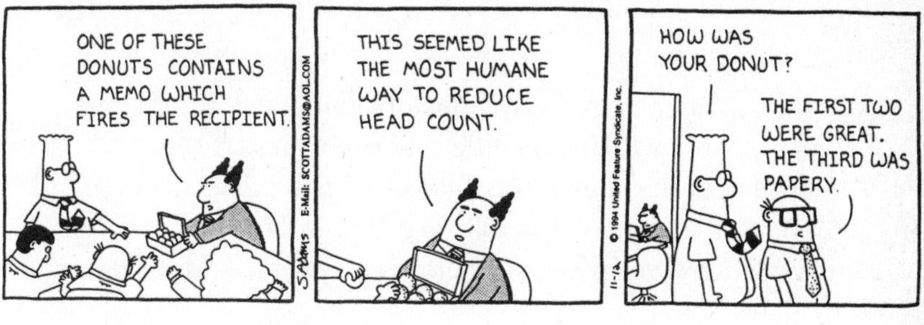
ONE OF THESE DONUTS CONTAINS A MEMO WHICH FIRES THE RECIPIENT.
E-Mail: SCOTTADAMS@AOL.COM
S. Adams
THIS SEEMED LIKE THE MOST HUMANE WAY TO REDUCE HEAD COUNT.
11-12
© 1994 United Feature Syndicate, Inc.
HOW WAS YOUR DONUT?
THE FIRST TWO WERE GREAT. THE THIRD WAS PAPERY.

COMPANIES THAT STILL HAVE TOO MANY EMPLOYEES

From: (name withheld)
To: scottadams@aol.com

Scott,

I spent Friday morning at [company's] quarterly all-hands meeting. I was willing to sacrifice a morning of my life for a T-shirt, in this case a very nice one.

Anyway, they gave out a "Process" award.

The award for best new process was awarded to the group who made up the process for awarding awards.

From: (name withheld)
To: scottadams@aol.com

Scott,

At my company we have a coordinator's committee for the five task forces that are working on office climate issues.

The mission of the committee is to coordinate the work of the task forces. The task of the task forces is to gather information and make recommendations on a process for creating a plan to address office climate issues . . .

I'm not making this up, as you obviously know!!

From: (name withheld)
To: scottadams@aol.com

Scott,

Last week, one of our managers called a meeting for all of the female personnel at one of our offices to say that someone has been stealing toilet paper from the women's room and that it has to stop.

Isn't that ludicrous? I mean, imagine the costs of this manager trying to monitor the toilet paper supply, and the costs of having several people attend this meeting when they could be working more productively. I'm sure the costs of this toilet paper policing and enforcement exceeds the costs of the few "stolen" rolls!

Well, it's not all for naught; this toilet paper scenario has somehow sparked some creative juices that our otherwise rule-laden, bureaucratic environment never does. In good humor, some people have started writing anonymous messages about it and someone has gone about the business of setting up another to be blamed for the stealing by placing a roll of toilet paper in another woman's desk drawer, and having a telltale end of it sticking out of the open drawer and rolled out onto the carpet and extending out of her cubicle! And of course all sorts of puns have emerged about wiping out the problem, etc.

From: (name withheld)
To: scottadams@aol.com

Scott,

I am not making this up.

At our company, our middle managers (two levels up) were all formed into an enormous committee to address areas of concern voiced by employees in one of our recent employee surveys.

There are about one hundred middle managers. They came up with many hilarious suggestions. This is the best one:

They formed a subcommittee to detect and excise "deadwood." Totally missing the fact that the definition of deadwood is "the other guy," they produced two suggestions:

(1) The Deadwood Hotline. Any employee could accuse any other employee of being "deadwood," upon which an investigation would be immediately launched. Paranoia.

(2) Groups of middle managers would "roam the halls," searching for deadwood. I call this the "Deadwood Posse." I have no idea how they intended this to work.

They failed the laugh test in front of the Executive Council, I'm happy to report.

From: (name withheld)
To: scottadams@aol.com

Scott,

Here's a copy of a REAL (no kidding!) memo which was sent out just a few days ago.

—Memo—

Over the past few months, the cost of our monthly donut meeting has been extremely high. Much of this cost is due to the fact that more and more donuts are needed at each meeting.

It's not that we have more people month to month, but because we are experiencing a lack of fairness when it comes to these donuts. For those employees who get to the meeting first, they are taking three or four donuts at a time, thus leaving nothing for the people who arrive a little later, therefore forcing the cafeteria to serve even more. In addition to this problem, there are people who normally do not attend the meeting just coming in for a donut or two. This needs to change.

Therefore, effective with the February meeting, and all subsequent meetings thereafter, we will be issuing a "Donut Ticket." This ticket will entitle the bearer to one twelve-ounce coffee or soda, and one piece of fresh fruit or a donut. We believe this will help eliminate excessiveness by our employees, and of course, keep our monthly cost down.

Our meetings are set for February 13th, 14th, and 15th– Before that time, please stop by the front desk to pick up your tickets for distribution to your departments. These tickets are to be distributed to the employees just before their meeting time. These tickets are not to be duplicated. These tickets are good for the "February Donut meeting only." One ticket per person, per meeting.

I appreciate your assistance in this matter. Should you have any questions, please do not hesitate to contact me.

—End of memo—

From: (name withheld)
To: scottadams@aol.com

Scott,

One delightful experience which you missed involved the critical strategies we incorporated in the Phase Group reports to the officers.

Clerical people transcribed the wonderful thoughts which group members scribed up on butcher paper taped to the wall. Some scribes didn't write all that clearly. A critical strategy was, "DON'T SELL PAST THE CLOSE." The transcription came out, "DON'T

SELL PLASTIC CLOTHES." We left it in the report. I think one intermediate-level manager picked up on it and questioned it. He let us leave it in.

From: (name withheld)
To: scottadams@aol.com

Scott,

Here is some fodder for you.

A programmer from the MIS Department wrote a useful program for Department A. Department A had a meeting with the MIS Department to have the program documented and enhanced. The MIS Department said the project could not be done.

Department A replied that the program already existed!

The next day Department A found that the program in question had been deleted from their computers.

The project was never done.

HOW DOWNSIZING IS ARTFULLY BEING HANDLED

From: (name withheld)
To: scottadams@aol.com

Scott,

I just got a company mailing saying that we'll have a "Special Day" where the people who are leaving the company for the Voluntary Force Reduction are supposed to sit in the cafeteria with name tags on and have the other employees wander around and look at them.
There's also supposed to be a bake sale. I'm not sure what the point is, but maybe if we make enough on the bake sale some of them could be rehired or something. I can't quite put my finger on why this seems kind of bizarre in a *Soylent Green* kind of way.

From: (name withheld)
To: scottadams@aol.com

Scott,

The large company I work for recently published guidelines for its new "Career Transition Plan" a.k.a. layoff policy.
This document has been sent to everyone in the company, which greatly boosted morale.
Among the "highlights and advantages" of this plan are that it is "competitive." This led me to think, "Hmmm. Is a competitive advantage of this company its Career Transition Plan? Should this layoff policy be included in recruiting interviews as an advantage of working here?"

From: (name withheld)
To: scottadams@aol.com

Scott,

I recently learned that in one of our executive meetings the vice president of the company made a presentation on the upcoming year's forecast. In the course of his speech he mentioned that the company would no longer have the position of marketing director.

You guessed it! The next person's turn to make a presentation was the director of marketing, and this was the way he was informed. Two weeks later he was gone.

I hope that didn't affect his presentation.

From: (name withheld)
To: scottadams@aol.com

Scott,

I had an abject lesson in corporate humiliation today. A whole slew of us here at [company] had to call a phone number to see if we were still employed. Management e-mailed a phone number, we called it—and got the elemental "thumbs up" or "you're meat."

Big yucks huh? Well, many folks commented on it all being reminiscent of Dilbert . . . In fact, my variant is: Boss sends out the 1–800-GOTJOB? number, *but* jobs are only available (in classic DJ style) to the seventh caller or whatever . . .

From: (name withheld)
To: scottadams@aol.com

Scott,

Morale is so bad in my department that they sent the "corporate shrink" down from [city]. He appeared to be depressed, probably because HIS job was being reengineered, and he didn't expect to keep his job another year.

He did a presentation to the work groups about things being tough all over . . . etc., but the gist of his message was: "Well if you think you've got it bad, listen to my story."

With a little bit of probing I found that the company insurance has no programs for other counseling—just the corporate shrink.

22

HOW TO TELL IF YOUR COMPANY IS DOOMED

You might be working for a company that is doomed. Check for the presence of any of these deadly factors:

<u>HARBINGERS OF DOOM</u>

- Cubicles

- Teamwork

- Presentations to management

- Reorganizations

- Processes

CUBICLES

Assuming your computer hasn't made you sterile, someday your descendants will look back and be amazed that people of our generation worked in things called "cubicles." They will view our lives much the way we now view the workers from the Industrial Revolution who (I've heard) worked twenty-three hours a day making steel products using nothing but their foreheads.

Imagine our descendants' disbelief when they read stories about how we were forced to sit in big boxes all day, enduring a stream of annoying noises, odors, and interruptions. They might think it was the product of some cruel experiment.

Scientist: "Whenever you start to concentrate, this device on the desk will make a loud ringing sound to stop you."

Employee: "Um. Okay."

Scientist: "If your stress levels begin to normalize we'll have your boss pop in and give you an assignment that sat on his desk until it was overdue."

Employee: "What exactly is this research supposed to discover?"

Scientist: "Nothing, really. We like to do this sort of thing to people during our lunch break."

The widespread use of cubicles is a direct result of early laboratory tests on rats.

In the early 1960s, rats were placed in a scale-model cubicle environment and given a set of unreasonable objectives. At first the rats scurried around excitedly looking for cheese. Eventually they realized that their efforts were not rewarded. The rats fell into a pattern of attending meetings and complaining about a lack of training. The researchers labeled these rats "poor team players" and ignored them. Many of the rats died or escaped, thus reducing headcount. Companies heard of this new method for reducing headcount and began moving employees into cubicles.°

If your company already has cubicles that doesn't necessarily mean it's doomed. But if the direction of the company is toward smaller cubicles or more people in each cubicle, you're doomed.

°Some companies kept the rats on the payroll, typically for jobs in auditing and Quality Assurance. If you suspect that your co-worker is a rat, observe his interaction with the computer mouse. If he is using it to manipulate the cursor, he's human. If he's trying to mate with it, he might be a holdover from earlier testing. If he's using it as a foot pedal, he's your boss.

TEAMWORK

HOW FOOLISH OF YOU TO HOST THE ALL-DAY STAFF MEETING AT YOUR HOUSE.
LET'S FORM SUB-TEAMS TO BE MORE EFFICIENT. TED WILL DO ACCIDENTAL SPILLS. ALICE, YOU CRITIQUE THE DECOR. I'LL BE A FLOATER.
KITCHEN, SHODDILY DONE...
I SPILLED MAYONNAISE ON THE WALL.
WHERE'S THE BATH-ROOM?
S. Adams E-Mail: SCOTTADAMS@AOL.COM
© 1994 United Feature Syndicate, Inc.

If you hear a lot of talk about teamwork at your company, you're doomed.

The whole concept of "teamwork" changed when it migrated from the world of sports to the world of business. In basketball, a good team player is somebody who passes the ball. If you put a businessperson on a basketball team he'd follow the player with the ball, saying things like "What do you plan to do with that? Can we talk about it first?"

HEY, WALLY, HOW DID YOU GET A ROOF FOR YOUR CUBICLE?
THIS STUFF IS ALL MODULAR. YOU JUST TAKE SOME IDIOT'S WALL AND MAKE IT YOUR CEILING.
BY ANY CHANCE, DO YOU KNOW WHAT HAPPENED TO MY WALL?
WHAT DID IT LOOK LIKE?

Teamwork is the opposite of good time management. You can't do a good job managing your time unless you can blow off your co-workers. They will try to convince you to abandon your priorities in favor of their priorities. They are selfish and evil.

When you're a team player you look like a big ol' pile of birdseed in an aviary. Every co-worker will swoop in for a beak full of your resources and leave you a little "present" that has limited resale value. Anywhere you see teamwork you'll see people with lots of beak wounds on their heads.

All companies experience some degree of teamwork, but they're not all doomed. An easy way to determine if you have enough teamwork to be doomed is simply to measure how long it takes from the time you decide to go to lunch together until the time you actually eat.

TIME IT TAKES TO GET TO LUNCH	TEAMWORK RATING
Five minutes	Teamwork is annoying but not yet dangerous
Fifteen minutes	Danger, Red Alert
Sixty minutes	Teamwork has reached critical mass; company doomed

PRESENTATIONS TO MANAGEMENT

Your company is doomed if your primary product is overhead transparencies. A typical company has just enough resources to do one of the following:

1. Accomplish something.

2. Prepare elaborate presentations that lie about how much is being accomplished.

The rational employee will divert all available resources away from accomplishing things and toward the more highly compensated process of lying about accomplishments. It's the same amount of work, but only one has a payoff.

REORGANIZATIONS

Managers are like cats in a litter box. They instinctively shuffle things around to conceal what they've done. In the business world this process is called "reorganizing." A normal manager will reorganize often, as long as he's fed.

You can tell that you've reorganized too often—and are therefore doomed—if you hear your co-workers asking any of these questions in the hallways:

"If I had to live in a dumpster, how bad would that be?"

"Where do street people shower?"

"Is tuberculosis fatal?"

SOMETIMES I THINK THESE CONSTANT REORGANIZATIONS ARE JUST EXCUSES FOR GETTING RID OF UNWANTED EMPLOYEES.
WHAT JOB DID YOU END UP WITH?
ORGAN DONOR.
MY SHOULDER IS ACTING UP. DO I TALK TO YOU OR IS THERE A FORM TO FILL OUT?
I DON'T THINK THAT'S AN "ORGAN."
E-Mail: SCOTTADAMS@AOL.COM
© 1994 United Feature Syndicate, Inc.

WE'RE GOING TO FOLLOW THE ADVICE OF THE DOGBERT CONSULTING COMPANY AND FORM "BATTLIN' BUSINESS UNITS."
WE'LL SPEND MOST OF OUR TIME CROSS-CHARGING AND UNDERMINING THE OTHER BBU'S.
A LITTLE COMPETITION IS HEALTHY.
WHATEVER YOU DO, DON'T TICK OFF THE JANITORIAL BBU.
E-mail: SCOTTADAMS@AOL.COM
© 1995 United Feature Syndicate, Inc. (NYC)

I'D LIKE EACH OF YOU TO GIVE ME A CURRENT RÉSUMÉ.
NOW, DON'T BE ALARMED. IT'S JUST SO THE NEW VP CAN GET TO KNOW YOU. IT'S NOT AN OBVIOUS PRELUDE TO MASSIVE STAFF CUTS.
SHOULD I BE WORRIED THAT YOU ALL HAVE A CURRENT RÉSUMÉ ON YOU?
DON'T WORRY. IT'S NOT AN OBVIOUS PRELUDE TO MASSIVE DISLOYALTY!
E-mail: SCOTTADAMS@AOL.COM
© 1995 United Feature Syndicate, Inc. (NYC)

UH... DILBERT, ABOUT THAT ASSIGNMENT I GAVE YOU LAST MONTH...
REMEMBER HOW YOU THOUGHT IT WAS A SILLY AND RIDICULOUS ASSIGNMENT?
YEAH?
WELL, IT TURNS OUT THAT I'VE BEEN SPONTANEOUSLY CHANNELING THE SPIRIT OF BOZO THE CLOWN.
© 1992 United Feature Syndicate, Inc.

PROCESSES

If your company is staffed with a bunch of boneheads, you are doomed. This situation is usually referred to indirectly as a need for "process improvement." If you notice a lot of attention being given to process improvement it's a sure sign that all the smart employees have left the company and those who remain are desperately trying to find a "process" that is so simple that the boneheads who remain can handle it.

At this point it would be very funny to close your eyes and imagine a public address system at your office with the following announcement: "Marilyn vos Savant has left the building."

I'M HAPPY TO REPORT THAT THE "EXCELLENCE IN TEAMING" READ-OUT IS NEARLY READY.
S. Adams E-mail: SCOTTADAMS@AOL.COM
IT'S TAKEN FORTY PEOPLE FROM A DOZEN DEPARTMENTS TO COMPLETE THE STUDY. WE FINALLY GOT COMPLETE BUY-IN.
© 1995 United Feature Syndicate, Inc. (NYC)
IS THAT THE STUDY OF WHY WE CAN'T MAKE DECISIONS?
ORIGINALLY. BUT IT EVOLVED INTO MORE OF A DISCUSSION OF SQUIRREL MIGRATION PATTERNS.
2/27

23

REENGINEERING

Reengineering was invented by Dr. Jonas Salk as a cure for Quality programs.

Just kidding.

The acknowledged parents of reengineering are Michael Hammer and James Champy. When I say they're the "parents" I don't mean they had sex—and I apologize for making you think about it. I mean they wrote the best-selling business book *Reengineering the Corporation*, which was published in 1993.

Businesses flocked to reengineering like frat boys to a drunken cheerleader. (This analogy wasn't necessary, but I'm trying to get my mind off that Hammer and Champy thing.)

Reengineering involves finding radical new approaches to your current business processes. On paper, this compares favorably with the "Quality" approach, which involves becoming more efficient at the things you shouldn't be doing.

But there is a dark side to reengineering. There's a risk that whatever natural incompetence is present in the company can be unleashed in epic scale instead of doled out in puny "Quality" portions. This can be dangerous if—as I've often stated—we're all a bunch of idiots.

Hammer noted this risk and cleverly followed up with another book in 1995, *The Reengineering Revolution*. It describes all the boneheaded things that managers did to screw up his recipe for reengineering.

Example of How to Screw Up Reengineering

CEO: "Underling, go reengineer the company."

Underling: "I'll need $2 million."

CEO: "For what?"

Underling: "I need it to reengineer the company."

CEO: "You fool—reengineering *saves* money."

Underling: "Um . . . I'll get right on it."

CEO: "Let me know when you're done."

Reengineering has a tendency to reduce the number of employees needed to perform a function. That unfortunate side effect causes fear and mistrust in the employees whose participation is vital to making reengineering a success. You might think fear and mistrust would sabotage the effort, but that doesn't have to be the case. There are many examples of processes that work just fine even when there's plenty of fear and mistrust. Examples:

- Capital punishment

- Presidential elections

- Multilevel marketing

From E-mail . . .

From: (name withheld)
To: scottadams@aol.com

Scott,

   In an executive washroom the other day I overheard this exchange:
   "Hey, how's it going? I haven't seen you in a while."
   "I got reengineered."
   "Hey, too bad."

Pity the poor slob who is assigned the task of reengineering the company; insufficient management support from above, treachery from below. It's possible to succeed, but the odds are against it.*

Here are some of the specific obstacles to reengineering.

SILVER BULLET DEFENSE

Managers are often asked to donate employees from their groups to the company's reengineering effort. This is an opportunity for managers to unload their most incompetent workers, all in the name of "teamwork." These incompetent employees act as "Silver Bullets" to destroy the reengineering project while leaving the existing organizations intact.

   Once the "Silver Bullets" are assembled it's time to have some meetings and brainstorm about radical reengineering options:

Silver Bullet #1: "Does anybody have any radical reengineering ideas?"

Silver Bullet #2: "Why don't we pre-lick all our envelopes?"

---

*The odds are approximately the same as if you bet on a race horse who has not won on a muddy track and it suddenly starts pouring rain. And the horse has a cast on two legs. And it's dead.

Silver Bullet #1: "That's more like an incremental "quality" idea than a radical "reengineering" idea."
(Long silence)

Silver Bullet #2: "We could downsize some people we don't know, thus saving money."

Silver Bullet #3: "Who would do their work?"
(Another long silence)

Silver Bullet #2: "Other people that we don't know?"

Silver Bullet #1: "I like those numbers!"

CAMOUFLAGE DEFENSE

Mid-level managers who are threatened by reengineering will make clever defensive adjustments. They quickly redefine whatever they're already doing as reengineering. Suddenly your "Customer Service Project" gets renamed to "Customer Service Reengineering Project." You're not getting a haircut, you're "reengineering your head." You're not going to lunch, you're "reengineering your intestines." Pretty soon there's so much reengineering going on that it's hard to find anything that *isn't* reengineering, at least in name.

Then comes budget time.

Senior executives know they should be funding something called "reengineering" or else they'll look like troglodytes. Reengineering is "in" and it's happening. The cheapest way to fund reengineering is by calling the stuff you're already funding "reengineering." (Senior managers were once middle managers; they know how to manage a budget.)

The executives might throw a bone to the one "real" reengineering project by giving it some money to do a small trial.

REENGINEERING TRIAL

A reengineering trial is a small-scale test of a proposed new "reengineered" process. Typically, none of the technology or resources that are proposed for the large-scale reengineering project is available for the trial. So planning for the trial goes like this:

Team Member #1: "We'll need distributed workstations, all connected by a worldwide satellite network system."

Team Member #2: "All we have is this pot of decaf coffee that was left here from the meeting before ours."

Team Member #3: "Let's use it. We can interpolate the results."

Team Member #1: "Are you nuts? That's *decaf*."

CONCLUSION

Reengineering a company is a bit like performing an appendectomy on yourself. It hurts quite a bit, you might not know exactly how to do it, and there's a good chance you won't survive it. But if it does work, you'll gain enough confidence to go after some of the more vital organs, such as that big red pumping thing.

TEAM-BUILDING
EXERCISES

If the employees in your company are a bunch of independent, antiso-
cial psychopaths, you might need some team-building exercises. Team-
building exercises come in many forms but they all trace their roots back
to the prison system. In your typical team-building exercise the employees
are subjected to a variety of unpleasant situations until they become either
a cohesive team or a ring of car jackers.

On two occasions during my cubicle career I had the thrill of participat-
ing in a "Ropes" course with my talented and trusted co-workers. I learned

so much in the first experience that the second Ropes course was much easier. In particular, I learned that if you fake a hand injury you can be exempt from activities that might kill you.

Our first "learning" during my second Ropes course experience was a trust-building exercise. We were randomly paired; one person would stand stiffly upright and fall backward, protected by the trusted partner who would break the fall. That seemed to work smoothly for most of the pairs in my group. But my partner (let's call her Margie) chose the path of least resistance and let gravity run its course. When quizzed about this later, Margie explained that she figured my wiry five-foot-eight-inch body would be "too heavy" so it was best to get out of the way.

I knew that later we would be expected to dangle from high trees protected only by the vigilance of our trusted co-workers who would be holding ropes to protect us. Sadly, my old hand injury flared up and I had to pass on that portion of event.

However, not all was lost in the experience. I did get to wear an incredibly dorky helmet and stand around watching my co-workers do things that aren't generally done by people who are—shall we say—smart enough to get out of jury duty. I felt quite majestic in my helmet, all outdoorsy, bonding with my teammates. Until somebody pointed out to the assembled crowd that my helmet was on backward. Another co-worker ran to get a camera because I "looked so funny" in my shorts and dorky helmet. That was the day I realized that if I ever tunneled out of that corporate prison hell I'd be sure to fill in the hole before sprinting for town.

The highlight of the experience for me was an exercise in which we had to move our entire team across a field, stepping only on log stumps that were placed too far apart for leaping. The trick was to use planks to build temporary bridges in just the right sequence to move the team without leaving any planks or people behind. Partway through this exercise our fearless district manager realized that listening to the opinions of the group was a losing strategy, so he "took control" and started barking directions. We followed his directions, even though they seemed to be somewhat suboptimal. But by then we trusted him—and of course there was always the "retribution thing" to worry about—so we readily accepted his leadership. The exercise ended with all of us except our leader safely on the other end of the field. He was stranded many stumps back trying to balance two planks in his arms. I think he's still there.

Everything else you need to know about team building and teamwork is in the cartoons and e-mail messages that follow.

TEAM WORK ILLUSTRATED

I HIRED RENOWNED PSYCHOLOGIST DOGBERT TO HELP US ACHIEVE PEAK PERFORMANCE IN TEAMWORK.
S. Adams E-mail: SCOTTADAMS@AOL.COM
PEAK PERFORMANCE IS SOMEWHAT RELATIVE. YOU'RE A HIGHLY DYSFUNCTIONAL TEAM,
SO WE MUST SET REALISTIC GOALS.
6/6 © 1995 United Feature Syndicate, Inc. (NYC)
WHAT WOULD BE A REALISTIC GOAL FOR US?
I THINK I CAN POSTPONE CANNABILISM.

DYSFUNCTIONAL TEAM...
I'D LIKE EVERYBODY TO TURN TO THE RIGHT AND SAY WHAT YOU ADMIRE ABOUT THAT PERSON.
S. Adams E-mail: SCOTTADAMS@AOL.COM
I ADMIRE YOUR LEATHERY SKIN, ALICE.
I ADMIRE YOUR ABILITY TO FIGURE OUT WHICH SIDE IS YOUR RIGHT IN ONLY TWO TRIES.
6/7 © 1995 United Feature Syndicate, Inc. (NYC)
I ADMIRE YOUR ABILITY TO GET PAID FOR THIS.
DESPITE THE FACT YOUR FACE SCARES CHILDREN, I ADMIRE YOUR CO-WORKERS.

IN THIS TEAM-BUILDING EXERCISE YOU WILL MAKE PAPER DOLLS WHILE BLINDFOLDED.
S. Adams E-mail: SCOTTADAMS@AOL.COM
THIS MAY SEEM ABSURD. BUT SOON, COGNITIVE DISSONANCE WILL SET IN AND YOU'LL CRY AND HUG AND THINK YOU LEARNED SOMETHING.
6/8 © 1995 United Feature Syndicate, Inc. (NYC)
ARE YOU SURE WE'LL CRY AND HUG?
ACTUALLY, HUGGING IS IFFY.

DYSFUNCTIONAL TEAM...
I'D LIKE EACH OF YOU TO TELL THE TEAM WHAT YOU LEARNED IN MY WORKSHOP.
S. Adams E-mail: SCOTTADAMS@AOL.COM
I LEARNED TO LISTEN WITH MY HEART. I GAINED RESPECT FOR OTHERS. I UNDERSTAND SANSKRIT. I GOT MY HAM RADIO LICENSE. I CAN DIVIDE BY ZERO...
6/9 © 1995 United Feature Syndicate, Inc. (NYC)
I LOVE GOING FIRST.

TALES OF TEAMWORK

From: (name withheld)
To: scottadams@aol.com

Scott,

At [company], a lot of business is done in the hallway. Getting dragged into these ad hoc meetings can be a huge time-waster; however, it's hard to avoid them because the participants always seem to want everyone's opinion.

I have taken to either excusing myself to the rest room to get out of them, or carrying ice back to my office from the kitchen by hand. That way, when I get caught in a meeting, I can say, "See, this ice is melting and my hand is cold. I must go now." They let me out, and nobody seems to question the utility or business case for my ferrying ice around all day.

From: (name withheld)
To: scottadams@aol.com

Scott,

So the team is hiring a new engineer, and we had a cube with furniture reserved for her. She's starting next week. But a guy on the team [Co-Worker #1] decided he'd rather have *that* cube than *his* cube, so he recruits some other team members to help him move in.

I come over to see what the fuss was about and they are just moving the new hire's furniture out. I sez to myself, "That furniture is better than my furniture," so I got the guys to move the new hire's furniture into my cube and take my furniture . . . well, actually my furniture ended up in [Co-Worker #1's] new cube, and his old furniture stayed where it was, which is now the new hire's cube.

As they're moving my desk, which is identical to [Co-Worker #1's] desk, out of my cube, another engineer [Co-Worker #2] comes by to see what the fuss was about, and happens to mention that that desk is better than *his* desk (because he hasn't got a desk, just a table).

So by the time the new hire shows up, I figure she'll have roughly two broken file cabinets, a four-by-four table, and a guest chair, and she'll be in the cube next to the conference area.

Plus, none of us worked at all this morning, and a couple people got pretty concerned that maybe one of us was leaving the team, what with our furniture being moved and all.

From: (name withheld)
To: scottadams@aol.com

Scott,

Here's a funny disaster scenario, a true situation that happened at a company I worked at. The president of our company decided we needed an off-site. He decided that an ideal off-site was a bike ride. He chose a thirty-mile route and handed out hand-drawn maps.

Half the company didn't have bikes and rented them. Nobody was in shape. The route turned out to be fairly hilly (and thirty miles is a long ride even in flat terrain for someone who doesn't ride regularly). The map was wrong and nobody had real maps. Several people got lost and never made it to lunch. One person ended up in the hospital (he collapsed due to low blood sugar while biking up a hill). The planned discussions and activities for the day never happened. And the president didn't understand until days later how much of a disaster the day had been. After all, he'd enjoyed his ride.

25

LEADERS

DEFINITION OF A LEADER

Leadership is an intangible quality with no clear definition. That's probably a good thing, because if the people being led knew the definition, they would hunt down their leaders and kill them.

Some cynics might say that a "leader" is a someone who gets people to do things that benefit the leader. But that can't be a good definition because there are so many exceptions, as you well know.*

---

*Please tell me what those exceptions are; I'm starting to get cynical.

ORIGIN OF THE WORD "LEADER"

The word "leader" is derived from the word "lead," as in the material that bullets are made out of. The term "leader" was popularized at about the same time as the invention of firearms. It grew out of the observation that the person in charge of every organization was the person whom everyone wanted to fill with hot lead.

I don't recommend this; it's just a point of historical interest.

LEADERSHIP VISION

Leaders spend their time concentrating on "visions" of the future. This can involve having lunch with other leaders, attending golf events, or even reading a book. It can take many forms, as long as nothing tangible is produced during the process. Through these activities the leader hopes to convince the employees of the following things:

1. The leader knows the future and has agreed to share it with the company instead of using this awesome power to make a fortune gambling.

2. The chosen direction is somehow not as "obvious" as you think, so you're lucky to have the leader at any price.

3. There are intangible benefits to being an employee. These intangible benefits compensate for the low pay and poor working conditions. The nature of these intangible benefits will be revealed to you at some future time, unless you have a bad attitude.

Obviously, any good leader operates under the assumption that the people being led are astonishingly gullible. This has proven to be a fair assumption throughout history, as demonstrated by the fact that many leaders have *not* been assassinated.

LEADER SURVIVAL SKILLS

The most important skill for any leader is the ability to take credit for things that happen on their own. In primitive times, tribal chieftains would claim credit for the change in seasons and the fact that wood floats. They had the great advantage of the ignorance of the masses working in their favor. But television has largely filled the "knowledge gap," so the modern leader must take credit for more subtle happenings.

For example, if the company accountants predict that profits are going up because of a change in international currency rates, the good leader will create a company-wide "Quality Initiative," thus having a program in place to take credit for the profit increase. The employees play along with the illusion in hopes that the leader will be noticed by another company and hired away. Everybody wins when the leader is successful.

WHERE DO LEADERS COME FROM?

It's an age-old question: Are leaders born or made? And if they're made can we return them under warranty?

Leaders are people who can pursue a path that is seemingly nonsensical or even dangerous to everybody else. Common sense tells us that nobody needs a leader to take the path that's intuitive; people would do that on their own. Therefore, since the leader recommends a path that is seemingly illogical to the "average" person, we can conclude that a leader must be either:

1. So smart that nobody can share the vision

Or . . .

2. A nitwit

To divine the answer to the "visionary or nitwit" question we can review some of the great acts of leadership and determine, after the fact, whether they were the work of the mentally incompetent or of great visionaries. If a pattern emerges, we have our answer.

GREAT WALL OF CHINA EXAMPLE

Take the Great Wall of China. It took literally dozens of Chinese people working overtime to build this wall that stretches for many miles across the Chinese nation. It's so large you can see it from outer space, although frankly it's not worth it because you'd have to hold your breath a long time and you'd probably burn up on reentry.

The Great Wall's purpose was to keep out invading armies. But invading armies soon realized that the gatekeepers along the Great Wall could easily be bribed. Thanks to unreasonable taxation by the Chinese rulers, the average gatekeeper's net worth was a crust of bread and a few shiny stones. This made the gatekeepers somewhat vulnerable to bribery.

Any invading general would pull his army up to the wall, toss a couple of sandals to the gatekeeper, and wait for the door to fling open. Then the general would kill the gatekeeper because there's no point in wasting good sandals.

Conclusion

The leaders who built the Great Wall were nitwits.

Secondary Conclusion

But they were smarter than gatekeepers.

GREAT PYRAMIDS EXAMPLE

Let's examine the great pyramids of Egypt. I've never actually watched an entire PBS show about the pyramids, so I can't speak authoritatively. But I think the purpose of the pyramids was to honor the leaders and maybe help them in the afterlife. It looked good on papyrus.

But it didn't turn out the way they planned. I once paid $12 to peer at the box that held King Tutankhamen's little bandage-covered midget corpse at the De Young Museum in San Francisco. I remember thinking how pleased he'd be about the way things turned out in his afterlife.

Conclusion

The leaders who built the pyramids were nitwits.

GENGHIS KHAN EXAMPLE

Many years ago, on a desperately cold evening on the tundra, Genghis Khan ordered his Mongol hordes to "mount their horses" and do a ride-by "mooning" of the neighboring village. There was no real reason for this except that he wanted some peace and quiet while he sat in his tent designing various fashion items made out of dead animals.

Some of the Mongols were later embarrassed to admit that they misinterpreted the order to "mount their horses." This made for a good laugh back at the camp.

Later, through a series of creative retellings, this whole Genghis Khan legend got blown up into a much bigger deal than it was. But you have to remember, there were maybe two dozen people on the planet at the time, so everything seemed important. And everybody agreed it was probably best to embellish the story a bit so the Mongol hordes wouldn't look bad in business books later on.

Conclusion

Genghis Khan was a nitwit as a leader, but he was a pretty fair designer of fur fashions.

MODERN EXAMPLES OF LEADERSHIP

One cannot reach a conclusion on the basis of a few historical examples, even if they do seem pretty darned persuasive. Let us turn instead to the words of some people who are being led in companies around the globe. I think you'll see a pattern emerge.

From: (name withheld)
To: scottadams@aol.com

Scott,

This is a true story:
Our overworked Accounting Department recently put in twenty straight days of work to close the books for the year, working through weekends and the 4th of July holiday. When it was over, one of the managers approached the big boss about possible comp time or money bonus. The boss replied, "Didn't you read the 'Red Badge of Courage'?" That was his full response.

From: (name withheld)
To: scottadams@aol.com

Scott,

Just when I thought management couldn't get any more
clueless . . .

A friend of mine here at [company] just turned in her resignation
letter today. Management red-penned it, and sent it back to her for a
rewrite (they thoughtfully provided her with a copy of the resignation
letter of her closest peer, who resigned last week, as a model of what
they liked to see).

By the way, both people mentioned "clueless management" as one
of the reasons they were leaving. They were challenged to provide
examples.

Duh . . .

From: (name withheld)
To: scottadams@aol.com

Scott,

A few years ago, the VPs of [company] visited a number of other
companies, with the purpose of discovering what management practices accounted for their success. One of the companies was Federal
Express.

After weeks and weeks of these visits, what did they come back
with? Well, it seems FedEx employees are called "associates," not
employees. That must be why FedEx does so well!

So it was announced to us with great fanfare that henceforth we
would all be called "associates," not employees. *All* of us would be
called associates, too—nice and egalitarian. This was supposed to

increase our efficiency and productivity. Some weeks later, the VP of human resources announced that now there would be "associates," "leaders" (i.e., supervisors and middle managers), and "senior leaders" (i.e., senior management).

This was the most visible (and the most effective) result of the VP's visits to see how to emulate well-run companies.

From: (name withheld)
To: scottadams@aol.com

Scott,

A recent work situation left me feeling totally Dilbert:

(1) Boss asks me what I think of a proposal he has because it impacts my department.

(2) I reply that I don't think it will work.

(3) Countless meetings, conference calls, and e-mails on the proposal.

(4) Consensus is that this is not a worthwhile proposal.

(5) Boss decides to implement proposal.

(6) Boss's boss e-mails boss asking why this proposal was implemented. It doesn't make sense.

(7) Boss forwards e-mail to me asking why we implemented proposal and to prepare a response!

From: (name withheld)
To: scottadams@aol.com

Scott,

Here's a true-life story.

I am working on a project in cooperation with [large company]. In this project we need to come up with a name of a [product]. They've had a lot of trouble deciding on a name.

Today we learned that they have made some real progress toward determining a name. Their management team explained that they have created a team of managers who will by next Monday identify another individual whose responsibility will be to produce a schedule for determining the name of the device.

And to think we were worried they weren't doing anything . . .

From: (name withheld)
To: scottadams@aol.com

Scott,

A newly appointed VP of my company, in an interview printed in the internal company news rag, made the following comment when asked whether existing employees would be relocated if the company won an upcoming contract, or if the company would instead hire local people:

"Engineers are basically a commodity. It doesn't make economic sense for the company to pay for moves when we can buy the same commodity on site."

Naturally, this disturbed some individuals in the workforce and a number of them showed up at an all-hands meeting held by this VP a few days later and sat in the front row plastered with signs labeling themselves as "Bananas," "Pork Bellies," etc.

The VP made a valiant effort to tap dance around his statements but didn't make many converts.

From: (name withheld)
To: scottadams@aol.com

Scott,

Look out, Newt . . .

My division has decided to inspire employees in true Republican style by giving each engineer a three-by-five-inch plastic card with the ten-point "[Division Name] Contract." According to a letter distributed with the contract:

"Someone once said that you know your strategy is sound if you can say 'no' to a request. Use this card in that way. If you're asked to do something not related to the contract, challenge its importance and sustain the focus we require to set ourselves up for a great future of opportunity, growth, and profit."

First of all, wasn't it *Dogbert* who noted the difference between a company with a strategy and one without a strategy?

Maybe life did imitate art in this case. You make the call. Take a look at this cartoon from a book published in 1991:

THE IMPORTANCE OF STRATEGIES

ALL COMPANIES NEED A
STRATEGY SO THE EMPLOYEES
WILL KNOW WHAT THEY
DON'T DO.

COMPANY WITH NO STRATEGY — UH-OH...WHAT SHOULD I DO? — RRRRING

COMPANY WITH A STRATEGY — WE DON'T DO THAT.

BUILD A BETTER LIFE BY STEALING OFFICE SUPPLIES Dogbert's Big Book of Business 101

From: (name withheld)
To: scottadams@aol.com

Scott,

This story is from a friend of mine who works for [company name].

Two senior-level VPs are scheduled to visit the lab. Of course all productive work is stopped for a week while the floors are buffed, the lab rearranged, and the bathrooms cleaned. (At least some good is coming out of this.)

One of the managers took it upon herself to label all of the equipment in the lab. She labeled everything short of the pencil sharpener. My friend actually removed some of the labels because at some point it was insulting.

Thank heavens there was a "Logic Analyzer" label covering the

HP Logic Analyzer logo. I think the label "Buffed Floor" wouldn't stick because of the new wax. The absurdity doesn't end here though.

A local VP takes a preview tour of the lab, shakes his head, and says, "Jesus, I wanted a lab tour not a trade show" and leaves. This creates a murmur in the powers-that-be:

"He didn't want a trade show." "He didn't want a trade show."

The final insult occurred as he was leaving and they were putting new sod down around the entrance in some of the more bare spots.

Another half day is lost while they rearrange the lab again.

I've got visions of an entourage including one guy to drop sod in front of these VPs lest someone's foot touch sand. I wonder how many people it takes to hold these guys off the toilet seats and how they fit them all into the stall???

From: (name withheld)
To: scottadams@aol.com

Scott,

The stupidest thing my boss ever did for our group was institute a point system. We all had checklists, and we checked off what we did during the day, and we got points.

Not a bright guy.

From: (name withheld)
To: scottadams@aol.com

Scott,

   True story:
   When we were down in the dumps one year, our newish CEO
decided that we needed a motivational meeting, complete with professional corporate motivation video. The video featured the "try
again until success" attitude of balloonist Maxie Anderson and was
coordinated with a personal letter from the famed balloonist.
   (Maxie had been killed three years earlier in a ballooning accident.)

From: (name withheld)
To: scottadams@aol.com

Scott,

   True story:
   One day at a meeting one of the big deals was daydreaming and
chewing on the side of his pen. The pen started leaking and no one
in the room bothered telling this guy that he had blue ink gathering
at the side of his lip and dripping on his shirt. Here they are trying to
keep a straight face and he has blue dripping down his face.
   They let him go the whole meeting that way.

From: (name withheld)
To: scottadams@aol.com

Scott,

Certain specific engineering disciplines are in demand around
here so experienced staff have been leaving for other companies to
make up to fifteen percent more money for about half the work.

Management calls a meeting of the remaining engineers.

There is some anticipation by these engineers that management
will announce some correction in their salaries or workload.

The meeting is held—management hands out T-shirts and basically says, "Have a nice day."

The engineers are seen in their offices dancing on the T-shirts.

From: (name withheld)
To: scottadams@aol.com

Scott,

You may not believe this; I didn't at first, but it is true.

A program here at [company] is requiring five hours per week
overtime. We do not get paid for the first five hours of overtime each
week. Anyway, a woman working on the program took two weeks of
vacation. When she returned she was told that she owed ten hours of
overtime for the time she did not put in while on vacation.

She told them they could fire her ass. I thought she was far too
nice about it.

From: (name withheld)
To: scottadams@aol.com

Scott,

Apparently, the Technical Division has sent around the new [company] Mission Statement and is requiring all the employees to sign it to indicate their support of it.

When you sign off on the Mission Statement, you get a special pin that you're supposed to wear. Then (here's the *best* part), if you see someone else wearing the special pin, you're supposed to give them the "secret salute." This "secret salute" consists of touching your hand to the pin and then giving the "thumbs up." We figured it would probably be easier to just give the Nazi salute.

Yours in Wonderland

From: (name withheld)
To: scottadams@aol.com

Scott,

We have a "Team Leader" here that also is one of those people (idiots) who comes into a meeting fifteen minutes late and insists on bringing up every topic that's already been discussed.

Over the holidays there wasn't much going on and he didn't have anything to do. He actually came into a meeting that had nothing to do with him or his department. He sat down and said he just didn't feel like he was "working" unless he could attend a meeting. Since this was the only meeting going on in the building that day, he decided to join it.

We agreed that he could sit there if he really felt the need, but only if he would keep quiet. Of course he couldn't, and brought up irrelevant points that we had already discussed.

From: (name withheld)
To: scottadams@aol.com

Scott,

Our company's eight-year "anniversary" was approaching. A bunch of employees got together to organize a party in the courtyard behind our building. When the boss found out he insisted on giving a speech during the festivities.

Well, everything went according to plan. Over a hundred employees showed up to eat fajitas and imbibe large amounts of margaritas. The boss then proceeds to get on his soapbox and give his speech, which consisted of "we may be a new company, but we will continue to become a better company by hopefully hiring better employees than we have now."

The amusing thing is that this man never realized he just insulted every employee in the company. We talk about the "infamous speech" to this day.

From: (name withheld)
To: scottadams@aol.com

Scott,

Is management at your company *this* inspired?
From the front page of [company's] Total Quality newsletter:
"The single factor that separates winning companies from their unsuccessful counterparts is the ability to stay competitive in an incredibly competitive world! . . ."

Does management have a firm grasp of the obvious or what . . . ??

From: (name withheld)
To: scottadams@aol.com

Scott,

Our director general gave an all-staff pep talk just before Christmas, at which he defined our mission as "being the company of choice for customers, partners, and employees," whereupon in February he resigned to go head up the competition.

Well, he certainly made his choice.

From: (name withheld)
To: scottadams@aol.com

Scott,

I was sitting here finishing my uncut raisin bagel and took the second to last bite . . . as I noticed a co-worker across the hall in the other cubicle saying something about "corporate executives" and not "walking the walk" . . . it occurred to me how perfectly the chunk of bagel in my hand would bounce off his head if I threw it full force across the cubes . . .

From: (name withheld)
To: scottadams@aol.com

Scott,

The story:

I created a graph a couple of years ago, showing a problem with a circuit that we had designed, and were using in most of our products. I had a meeting with our VP of Engineering, and during the meeting I told him that we had a problem, and I showed him the graph.

He took the graph, looked at it, and said, "Wow."

I thought he was seeing the same thing I was: There was a problem with the circuit, and we would have to fix it in a substantial part of our product line.

"Wow," he said again, "How did you make this graph?"

Over the next two weeks, I spent most of my time creating graphs for our VP of Engineering to use in his Corporate Management Committee meetings, where he was finally able to upstage all the marketing bozos (other VPs) with their Mac graphics that their secretaries had spent a week working on.

If I had drawn the graph on a piece of engineering paper, then he might have seen the problem, and we might have fixed it. As it was, though, I did not work on the problem until a year later, when our customers finally tracked down a problem they were having, and found that it was in our chip (the same problem), and demanded that we fix it.

Oddly enough (or maybe not), I then got credit not for finding the problem before our customers had trouble with the part, but for fixing it after the customers found it.

From: (name withheld)
To: scottadams@aol.com

Scott,

A manager suggested a way to keep meetings on time:

For every minute late to a meeting the tardy person has to contribute $1 for every person present and kept waiting.

($ = persons x minutes).

This did not last long as soon as the instigator of this policy arrived forty minutes late to a meeting with thirty people!

From: (name withheld)
To: scottadams@aol.com

Scott,

In our company, we were required to account for our time on our time cards in °°SIX MINUTE INCREMENTS°°. Mind you, we were supposedly "salaried" employees.

The reason for this pickiness is that some years ago, division potentates were caught messing with the books. The cure for this was not to particularly punish the princes, but rather to flog the peasants by harassing them about every detail of their time charges (we have eleven-digit charge numbers).

A while back, one of our people was caught in a sneak audit. Questions like, "What are you working on? What is your charge number? Have you ever committed fraud?" (Not kidding about the last. They DO ask!!)

But the interview lasted longer than six minutes . . . (just seven minutes, to be exact). So later on he was called on the carpet for charging the interview time to his project!! The worker had to write a memo saying he was sorry, the supervisor had to write a memo saying it would never happen again, and the "cognizant VP" (an evident oxymoron) wrote a memo saying heads would roll if this flagrant misbehavior continued. . . .

Things are improving, though: They relaxed the rules so we now only have to account for our time in fifteen-minute intervals . . .

From: (name withheld)
To: scottadams@aol.com

Scott,

Recently, a human resources manager was telling me about an employee that was having trouble with repetitive stress syndrome and it was related to using a mouse. I suggested that person be given a $150 pen and tablet to replace the mouse and alleviate pain while restoring productivity.

The manager's response was, "Shhhh, don't tell anyone about this. If they find out that they can avoid pain and suffering, everyone will want one of these things!"

From: (name withheld)
To: scottadams@aol.com

Scott,

During a particularly vicious interoffice war, when everyone was sweating for their jobs, the director walks into the weekly staff meeting, places a tape recorder on the table, and turns it on. Everyone sits up, glances right and left. Expressions go carefully vacant.

The director berates the attendees for not speaking up in meetings and for being "too stressed out."

Then the director's hench-person passes out copies of a form labeled "STRESS-O-METER." The form has seven boxes, each labeled with a degree of stress. The names went all the way from "don't care about anything" (zero stress) to "ready to explode" (number seven stress).

Each form had to be filled out, signed, and returned.

The STRESS-O-METERS were collected, totaled, averaged, and the number posted on an office wall.

"Stress at 4.3 this week!"

Next week, "Stress at 4.2, good work!"

Of course, all the "confidential" forms were taped to the coffee room wall, so everyone tried to figure out who was ready to explode and who was sleeping in their office.

From: (name withheld)
To: scottadams@aol.com

Scott,

So here's the latest from my company:

Our systems organization has recently gone through a series of layoffs, each supposedly final. Whole groups have been outsourced, but only after lengthy and public debate of how their detailed technical knowledge is "non-value-added." There is an ongoing "Bullet Team" to try to implement the "Indian Initiative." We have just reorganized, and half of the management has been appointed very obviously on the basis of their ability to suck up to the guy in charge of that half.

Morale is just a wee bit low.

Now, surprisingly enough, the morale problem has been acknowledged. (I think they're a little worried that people are starting to leave without being laid off first.) A "Work-Out" was called to address the issue. Alternatives discussed at the Work-Out included:
- Recognizing and rewarding technical expertise.
- Getting a pay scale close to market value.
- Communicating outsourcing plans and guidelines.
- Retraining folks with those less "value-added" skills.

After all those alternatives (and many more) were discussed, the outcome of lengthy deliberation was . . . The FUN Team!!! Employee morale is low. We need more picnics and bowling. If we just socialize more, all our problems will go away.

If I had just gone to more leadership classes, I'm sure I'd understand all this. . . .

THE IMPORTANCE OF HAIR FOR MALE LEADERS

Lastly, no discussion of leadership can be complete without considering hair. For women, it's sufficient just to have hair. But for men, the quality of hair is an essential leadership component.

The hair-leadership correlation is something I first noticed while working at Crocker Bank and then later at Pacific Bell. Over time I realized it couldn't be a coincidence.

At the top of the executive heap you consistently find men with thick, medium-length, parted-at-the-side hair. It's the kind of hair that turns silver with time, never thinning. Perma hair. Jack Kemp hair. Newt Gingrich hair. Hair that will not die. Hair that can deflect a bullet. Hair that would protect a space vehicle on reentry.*

---

*In case you want to go look at the Great Wall of China.

There are exceptions, of course. Sometimes a highly capable bald executive like Barry Diller will slip through, like a dolphin evading a tuna net. But this is rare and I attribute it mostly to the fact that these executives are part dolphin. (If you look closely at Barry Diller you'll see a little blow hole right on the top of his head.) The executives who are part dolphin can be identified by two striking characteristics:

1.   They lack hair.

2.   They ask you to write a "porpoise statement."

CONCLUSION

I don't mean for this chapter to imply that leadership is the same as a con job. The differences are substantial, in the sense that leadership pays much more and doesn't require quick wits. I recommend it as a career path to all of you.

LEADERSHIP ILLUSTRATED

THE COMPANY HAS ANNOUNCED THERE WILL BE NO RAISES OR PROMOTIONS THIS YEAR.
NOW, THERE'S A MATHEMATICAL CERTAINTY THAT NO MATTER HOW HARD YOU WORK, INFLATION WILL MAKE YOU POORER.
I HATED THE OLD WAY, WITH ALL THE UNCERTAINTY.
I'M NOT JUST A MANAGER, I'M A LEADER!
S. Adams
E-Mail: SCOTTADAMS@AOL.COM
3-10
© 1994 United Feature Syndicate, Inc.

AS THE LEADER OF THIS ORGANIZATION, IT'S MY JOB TO SET PRIORITIES.
HERE'S YOUR CALENDAR. I BOOKED YOU THROUGH NEXT YEAR WITH EVERY YAHOO WHO COULD DIAL YOUR NUMBER.
MAYBE I'LL CALL THIS A PRIORITY.
2-16
S. Adams
E-Mail: SCOTTADAMS@AOL.COM
© 1994 United Feature Syndicate, Inc.

Dilbert
By Scott Adams
CONGRATULATIONS!
YOU'VE BEEN NAMED "FLOOR WARDEN."
IN THE EVENT OF A FIRE WE'LL RELY ON YOUR LEADERSHIP TO GET US OUT SAFELY.
LET ME SEE IF I UNDERSTAND THIS...
YOU'RE THE LEADER WHEN IT INVOLVES UNINFORMED DECISIONS IN RETURN FOR HUGE STOCK OPTIONS.
BUT I'M THE LEADER WHEN IT COMES TO RISKING DEATH IN A HIGHRISE INFERNO WHILE YOU SCRAMBLE OVER THE ASHEN BACKS OF FALLEN CO-WORKERS.
WHAT MAKES YOU THINK YOUR LIFE IS WORTH MORE THAN MINE?
I'VE GOT STOCK OPTIONS AND YOU'RE A FLOOR WARDEN.
DON'T EXPECT ANY CPR.
E-Mail: SCOTTADAMS@AOL.COM
S. Adams
1-8

CAN YOU EXPLAIN WHY YOU'RE A WEEK BEHIND SCHEDULE?
YOUR POOR LEADERSHIP HAS DRAINED ME OF THE ENTHUSIASM THAT IS NECESSARY TO SUCCEED. BUT IT'S NOT COMPLETELY YOUR FAULT.
FRANKLY, YOUR PARENTS HAVE TO ACCEPT SOME RESPONSIBILITY FOR CREATING YOU.
EVEN IF THEY WERE DRUNK?
S. Adams E-mail: SCOTTADAMS@AOL.COM
© 1995 United Feature Syndicate, Inc. (NYC)

MY NEW STYLE OF MANAGEMENT IS EXHAUSTING ME.
I HEARD SOME PEOPLE TALKING ABOUT "MBWA" OR "MANAGEMENT BY WALKING AROUND."
I WALKED ALL THE WAY TO THE PARK AND BACK. BUT I CAN'T SAY THAT I SEE MUCH IMPROVEMENT AROUND HERE.
S. Adams
Internet: scottadams@aol.com

I'M TOLD BY A RELIABLE SOURCE THAT OUR SENIOR VICE PRESIDENT MADE A SOUND LIKE "YURP" AT LUNCH.
WHAT DOES IT MEAN? DOES IT SIGNAL A NEW SET OF PRIORITIES? WE MUST DEMONSTRATE OUR COMMITMENT TO THIS VISION.
WHAT WAS THE CONTEXT OF THIS VISION?
ALL WE KNOW IS HE WAS EATING A BURRITO.
S. Adams E-Mail: SCOTTADAMS@AOL.COM

WE'VE REDESIGNED THE ORGANIZATION CHART TO SHOW MANAGEMENT AT THE BOTTOM SUPPORTING OUR MOST IMPORTANT EMPLOYEES!
QUESTION: WHY DO THE MOST IMPORTANT EMPLOYEES GET PAID THE LEAST?
BECAUSE THEY WOULD NEVER THINK OF IDEAS LIKE THIS UPSIDE-DOWN CHART CONCEPT.
S. Adams E-Mail: SCOTTADAMS@AOL.COM

WE'VE STUDIED THE JAPANESE MODEL AND DECIDED TO COPY THEIR BEST PRACTICES.
LONG TERM INVEST-ING?
KARAOKE!
SHAFT! CAN YOU DIG IT?
THANK GOD WE DON'T HAVE LIFETIME EMPLOY-MENT.
S. Adams E-Mail: SCOTTADAMS@AOL.COM
12-5 © 1994 United Feature Syndicate, Inc.

UH-OH... THE MANAGERS ARE GOING TO ANOTHER CLOSED-DOOR MEETING.
IT MUST BE ABOUT PAY CUTS OR LAYOFFS. I'M DOOMED. I'D BETTER WORK ON MY RÉSUMÉ NOW.
OKAY, SO FAR OUR "LEADERSHIP VISION" SAYS "WE INSPIRE EMPLOYEES TO ACTION." DOES ANYBODY HAVE UPGRADES?
NAH
S. Adams E-mail: SCOTTADAMS@AOL.COM
3-11 © 1995 United Feature Syndicate, Inc. (NYC)

DID YOU REMEMBER WHAT THE STEERING COMMITEE DECIDED ABOUT MY PROJECT?
NOPE.
YOU'D BETTER CALL A MEETING WITH ALL THE DEPARTMENT HEADS. THEIR ORDERS WILL OVERRIDE THE STEERING COMMITEE AND MAKE IT A MOOT POINT.
IT WILL TAKE MONTHS TO GET ON ALL OF THEIR CALENDARS.
AND DON'T INVITE YOUR-SELF. IT'S FOR LEADERS ONLY.
5-23 S. Adams E-Mail: SCOTTADAMS@AOL.COM
© 1994 United Feature Syndicate, Inc.

OUR CEO WILL VISIT HERE NEXT WEEK. YOU ALL KNOW WHAT TO DO.
WE SHOULD STOP ALL PRODUCTIVE WORK AND CREATE OVERHEAD TRANSPARENCIES THAT EXAGGERATE OUR VALUE.
AND A FEW OF OUR UGLIER CO-WORKERS WILL BE REPLACED BY ACTORS.
AS LONG AS IT'S NOT GERARD DEPARDIEU.
S. Adams E-Mail: SCOTTADAMS@AOL.COM 7-28
© 1994 United Feature Syndicate, Inc.

BOSS TYPES
FIND YOUR BOSS ON THIS HANDY REFERENCE.
S. Adams E-Mail: SCOTTADAMS@AOL.COM
HOSTAGE TAKER: TRAPS YOU IN YOUR CUBICLE AND TALKS YOUR EARS OFF.
BLAH BLAH
OW!!
FRAUD: USES VIGOROUS HEAD-NODDING TO SIMULATE COMPREHENSION.
THEN WE'LL SUBNET OUR IP ADDRESSES.
OH YEAH OH YEAH
MOTIVATIONAL LIAR: HAS NO CLUE WHAT YOU DO BUT SAYS YOU'RE THE BEST.
NOBODY CAN DO WHAT YOU DO!!
EXCEPT A MUSHROOM.
OVER PROMOTED: TRIES TO MASK INCOMPETENCE WITH POOR COMMUNICATION.
LET'S QUALITIZE OUR PARADIGM SO WE DON'T OVER INUNDATE WITH DATUMS.
© 1995 United Feature Syndicate, Inc.
WEASEL: TAKES CREDIT FOR YOUR HARD WORK.
THIS BONUS IS FOR BRILLIANTLY FORCING YOUR STAFF TO WORK 80 HOUR WEEKS.
IT WASN'T EASY!
2-19
MOSES: ,PERPETUALLY WAITS FOR CLEAR SIGNALS FROM ABOVE.
DON'T DO ANYTHING IMPORTANT YET.
NEVER HAVE.
PERFECT BOSS: DIES OF NATURAL CAUSES ON A THURSDAY AFTERNOON.
SHOULD WE DO SOMETHING?
THREE DAY WEEKEND!

26

NEW COMPANY MODEL: OA5

In this chapter you will find a variety of untested suggestions from an author who has never successfully managed anything but his cats. (And now that I think of it, I haven't seen the gray one for two days.)

Some people think that because I cleverly mock current management methods I must have some excellent ideas that I am selfishly keeping to myself. Over time, I have begun to believe this myself. (If this doesn't prove my central thesis—that we're all idiots—then nothing will.)

I doubt that anything you read here will improve your life, but I'm fairly confident that it won't hurt you either, and that's better than a lot of the things you're doing now.

If any of you are gullible enough to take my recommendations, don't say you weren't warned. That said, I think you'll find some interesting ideas here.

FUNDAMENTALS

The key to good management is knowing what's fundamental to success and what's not. Here's my grand insight about company fundamentals:

Companies with effective employees and good products usually do well.

Ta-daa!!

That might seem like a blinding flash of the obvious, but look around your company and see how many activities are at least one level removed from something that improves either the effectiveness of the people or the quality of the product.* (Note: If you're in one of those jobs, you might want to update your résumé.)

Any activity that is one level removed from your people or your product will ultimately fail or have little benefit. It won't seem like that when you're doing it, but it's a consistent pattern.

It's hard to define what I mean by being "one level removed" but you know it when you see it. Examples help:

- If you're writing code for a new software release, that's fundamental, because you're improving the product. But if you're creating a policy about writing software then you're one level removed.

- If you're testing a better way to assemble a product, that's fundamental. But if you're working on a task force to develop a suggestion system then you're one level removed.

- If you're talking *to* a customer, that's fundamental. If you're talking *about* customers you're probably one level removed.

- If you're involved in anything on the list below, you're one level removed from the fundamentals of your company and you will not be missed if you are abducted by aliens.

NOT FUNDAMENTAL

Quality Faire
Process Improvement Team

---

*When I refer to "product" I mean the entire product experience from the customer's perspective, including the delivery, image, and channel.

      Recognition Committee
      Employee satisfaction survey
      Suggestion system
      ISO 9000
      Standards
      Policy improvement
      Reorganization
      Budget process
      Writing Vision Statements
      Writing Mission Statements
      Writing an "approved equipment list"

These "one off" activities are irresistible. You can make a convincing argument for all of them. You couldn't run a company, for example, without a budget process. I'm not suggesting you try. But I think you can focus more of your energy on the fundamentals (people and product) by following a simple rule for all the "one off" activities.

Rule for "one off" activities: consistency. Resist the urge to tinker. It's always tempting to "improve" the organizational structure, or to rewrite the company policy to address a new situation, or to create committees to improve employee morale. Individually, all those things seem to make sense. But experience shows that you generally end up with something that is no more effective that what you started with.

For example, companies tinker endlessly with the formula for employee compensation. Rarely does this result in happier and more productive employees. The employees redirect their energies toward griping and preparing résumés, the managers redirect their energies toward explaining and justifying the new system.

The rule of consistency would direct you toward keeping your current compensation plan—warts and all—unless it's a true abomination. The company that focuses on fundamentals will generate enough income to make any compensation plan seem adequate.

The best example of a fruitless, "one off" activity that seems like a good idea is the reorganization. Have you ever seen an internal company reorganization that dramatically improved either the effectiveness of the employees or the quality of the product?

Sometimes there are indirect benefits because a reorganization is a good excuse for weeding out the ninnies, but that hardly justifies the disruption. The rule of consistency would say it's best to keep the organization as it is, unless there's a fundamental shift in the business. Add or subtract people as needed, but leave the framework alone. Let the employees spend time on something besides reordering business cards.

Many of the "one off" activities start taking care of themselves if you're doing a good job with your people and your products. A company with a good product rarely needs a Mission Statement. Effective employees will suggest improvements without being on a Quality Team. Nobody will miss the Employee Recognition Committee if the managers are effective and routinely recognize good performance. The budget process will suddenly look very simple if you're making money (by focusing on your products).

As far as consistency goes, I would make an exception for changes that are radical enough to qualify as "reengineering" a process. It's the fiddling I object to, not elimination or major streamlining.

If you buy my argument that too much energy is being spent on the "one off" activities, the next question is how to focus on the fundamentals of making your people more effective and your products more desirable.

I'm here to help.

OUT AT FIVE

I developed a conceptual model for a perfect company. The primary objective of this company is to make the employees as effective as possible. I figure the best products usually come from the most effective employees, so employee effectiveness is the most fundamental of the fundamentals.

The goal of my hypothetical company is to get the best work out of the employees and make sure they leave work by five o'clock. Finishing by five o'clock is so central to everything that follows that I named the company OA5 (Out at Five) to reinforce the point. If you let this part of the concept slip, the rest of it falls apart. You'll see why.

In today's corporate environment the employee who walks out the door at five P.M. is held in lower regard than a Michael Jackson Day Care Center. The goal of OA5 is to change that—to guarantee that the employee who leaves at five P.M. has done a full share of work and everybody realizes it. For that to happen, the OA5 company has to do things differently than an ordinary company.

Companies use a lot of energy trying to increase employee satisfaction. That's very nice of them, but let's face it—work sucks. If people liked work they'd do it for free. The reason we have to pay people to work is that work is inherently unpleasant compared to the alternatives. At OA5 we recognize that the best way to make employees satisfied about their work is to help them get away from it as much as possible.

An OA5 company isn't willing to settle for less productivity from the employees, just less time. The underlying assumptions for OA5 are:

- Happy employees are more productive and creative than unhappy ones.

- There's a limit to how much happiness you can get while you're at work. Big gains in happiness can only be made by spending more time away from work.

- The average person is only mentally productive a few hours a day no matter how many hours are "worked."

- People know how to compress their activities to fit a reduced time. Doing so increases both their energy and their interest. The payoff is direct and personal—they go home early.

- A company *can't* do much to stimulate happiness and creativity, but it can do a lot to kill them. The trick for the company is to stay out of the way. When companies try to encourage creativity it's like a bear dancing with an ant. Sooner or later the ant will realize it's a bad idea, although the bear might not.

STAYING OUT OF THE WAY

Most people are creative by nature and happy by default. It doesn't seem that way because modern management is designed to squash those impulses. An OA5 company is designed to stay out of the way and let the good things happen. Here's how:

1. Let the employees dress any way they want, decorate their work spaces any way they want, format memos any way they want. Nobody has ever demonstrated that these areas have an impact on productivity. But when you "manage" those things you send a clear signal that conformity is valued above either efficiency or creativity. It's better to get out of the way and reinforce the message that you expect people to focus on what is important.

   I stop short of recommending that employees should use any kind of computer that they want. Every situation is different, but there can be overriding efficiency considerations for keeping a standard computer type. Efficiency has to be a higher principle than creativity, otherwise you have chaos.

2. Eliminate any artificial "creativity" processes in the company, such as the Employee Suggestion Plan or Quality Teams. Creativity comes naturally when you've done everything else right. If you have a good e-mail system, a stable organization chart, and an unstressed workplace the good ideas will get to the right person without any help. The main thing is to let people know that creativity is okay and get out of the way.

WHAT DOES AN OA5 MANAGER DO?

"Staying out of the way" isn't much of a job description for a manager. So if you want to be a manager in an OA5 company you'll need to do some actual work too. Here are the most useful activities I can think of for a manager.

1. Eliminate the assholes. Nothing can drain the life-force out of your employees as much as a few sadistic assholes who seem to exist for the sole purpose of making life hard for others.

Sadly, assholes often have important job skills that you'd like to keep. My advice is that it's never worth the tradeoff. In an OA5 company if you're making your co-workers unhappy, then you're incompetent by definition. It's okay to be "tough" and it's okay to be "aggressive" and it's okay to disagree—even shout. That's not necessarily being an asshole. Some conflict is healthy. But if you do it with disrespect, or you seem to be enjoying it, or you do it in every situation, guess what—you're an asshole. And you're gone.

2. Make sure your employees are learning something every day. Ideally, they should learn things that directly help on the job, but learning anything at all should be encouraged. The more you know, the more connections form in your brain, and the easier every task becomes. Learning creates job satisfaction and supports a person's ego and energy level. As an OA5 manager you need to make sure every person is learning something every day. Here are some ways you can ensure that people are learning daily:

- Support requests for training even when not directly job related.

- Share your own knowledge freely and ask others to do the same, ideally in small digestible chunks.

- Make trade magazines and newspapers available.

- If the budget allows, try to keep employees in current computers and software. Make Internet connections available.

- Support experimentation sometimes even when you know it's doomed (if the cost is low).

- Make "teaching" a part of everybody's job description. Reward employees who do a good job of communicating useful information to co-workers.

3. Collectively all the little things create an environment that supports curiosity and learning. Imagine a job where after you've screwed up your boss says "What did you learn?" instead of "What the hell were you thinking?"

4. Teach employees how to be efficient. Lead by example, but also continuously reinforce the following behaviors in others:

- Do creative work in the morning and do routine, brainless work in the afternoon. For example, staff meetings should be held in the afternoon (if at all). This can have a huge impact on people's actual and perceived effectiveness.

- Keep meetings short. Get to the point and get on. Make it clear that brevity and clarity are prized. The reward for brevity is the ability to leave at five o'clock with a clear conscience. Every company says brevity is good but only an OA5 company rewards it directly.

- Blow off low-priority activities and make it clear why. Don't be sucked into an activity because it's the polite thing to do. If it's a "one off" activity, say no. Say why you're saying no. Be direct.

- Respectfully interrupt people who talk too long without getting to the point. At first it will seem rude. Eventually it gives everybody permission to do the same, and that's a tradeoff that can be appreciated. Remember, there's a reward—you get out at five.

- Be efficient in the little things. For example, rather than have some Byzantine process for doling out office supplies, add $25 a month to each employee's paycheck as a "supply stipend" and let employees buy whatever they need from their local store. If they spend less, they keep the difference.

- If you create an internal memo with a typo, just line it out and send it. Never reprint it. Better yet, stick with e-mail.

THE BIG FINISH

A culture of efficiency starts with the everyday things that you can directly control: clothes, meeting lengths, conversations with co-workers, and the like. The way you approach these everyday activities establishes the culture that will drive your fundamental activities.

What message does a company send when it huddles its managers together for several days to produce a Mission Statement that sounds something like this:

"We design integrated world-class solutions on a worldwide basis."

Answer: It sends a message that the managers can't write, can't think, and can't identify priorities.

Managers are obsessed with the "big picture." They look for the big picture in Vision Statements and Mission Statements and Quality Programs. I think the big picture is hiding in the details. It's in the clothes, the office supplies, the casual comments, and the coffee. I'm all for working on the big picture, if you know where to find it.

Finally—and this is the last time I'm going to say it—we're all idiots and we're going to make mistakes. That's not necessarily bad. I have a saying: "Creativity is allowing yourself to make mistakes. Art is knowing which ones to keep."

Keep your people fresh, happy, and efficient. Set a target, then get out of the way. Let art happen. Sometimes idiots can accomplish wonderful things.

TALES OF COMPANIES THAT TURN ON THEMSELVES

Here are some of my favorite stories of employees who need to be weeded out.

From: (name withheld)
To: scottadams@aol.com

Scott,

Let me relate an incident that typifies a bizarre trait of the "squirrel" human condition.

Desperate to resolve a bad customer problem with a dead system, the techie finally isolates the cause and needs a replacement widget.

It is after hours. Using every informal channel he knows, he finally tracks down the emergency store man who, surprisingly, isn't too miffed about the late-night call. They read the runes (microfiche), find the right part number, check the stores database, and find one in a depot close by.

"Great—that's a relief!"

"Whoa—I can't let you have THAT."

"Why not!?" (Mounting hysteria . . .)

"That's the last one—if I let you have that, I'd be out of stock!"

. . . agonized scream cut short by dial tone . . .

From: (name withheld)
To: scottadams@aol.com

Scott,

I have yet to convince anyone that the following actually happened.

Shortly after taking my first job, I submitted a trip report and expense account only to have it returned to my desk because one item "violated company policy." Being a concerned employee, I immediately contacted the soon-to-be-retired career bureaucrat in charge, expressed my contrition, and requested a copy of the company policies so as to avoid another violation. The bureaucrat informed me that company policies were secret and not for general distribution, as then "everyone would know them."

After a moment of silent contemplation, I slunk back to my desk, realizing that I was clearly outclassed.

From: (name withheld)
To: scottadams@aol.com

Scott,

The MIS manager, who doesn't know anything about computers, buys computers one at a time so he can purchase them on his personal credit card. He then files for reimbursement on his expense account. Why does he do this? To acquire frequent flyer miles given by his credit card company. Therefore, it takes an entire year to buy twenty computers.

From: (name withheld)
To: scottadams@aol.com

Scott,

This happened to one of my cubie-mates.

He uses a Daytimer to keep track of appointments, deadlines, etc. This being December, he went (as he has each previous December) to the "Supply Sergeant" (our director's secretary) to get his refill. She informed him that she had only ordered for "management" (of which he was not) and a few others. Obviously, he was not on that list either.

However, he was told that if he were to bring his old one ('94) to her (in order to prove that he does use it), she would give him a new insert.

His response . . . "Thanks anyway, I'll find some other way to keep my notes and appointments." Being the inventive software engineer that he is, he now has numerous paper towels (from the rest room) hanging from his desk bookshelf.

From: (name withheld)
To: scottadams@aol.com

Scott,

I'm currently a senior software engineer at [company]. I'm rather young (twenty-four), so am looked down upon by one of our more "experienced" engineers.

During a design meeting I was running, this guy stood up and started saying I was completely off base and what I was proposing would never work. When asked for an alternative he went barreling off into a confused discussion of a different topic. He finally declared that we had to do things his way even though "his way" was a rather unclear concept, and did not address our design problem.

When asked to justify his position, the man replied, "I have years of experience." When pressed for a more descriptive justification he clarified things a bit. "I have years of experience—you wouldn't understand."

Needless to say he wasn't invited to future meetings.

From: (name withheld)
To: scottadams@aol.com

Scott,

True story:

A customer requests a product and we order it for him. The guy in shipping says okay and enters them into his database. After a few days, the customer calls to ask where his order is. We call to shipping and the shipper guy says, "Oh yeah, I couldn't find the customer in my database so I canceled the order." (Of course, without telling anybody.) So we ask the shipping guy to search his database right now for the ORDER NUMBER he gave us. He responds, "Nope, I can't find that customer's name in my database." So then we ask him "Okay, now try searching on the ORDER NUMBER you gave us." He says, "Oh, here it is–yeah, it says I canceled that order because I couldn't find them in the database." Hmmm.

From: (name withheld)
To: scottadams@aol.com

Scott,

Our company is so bad we actually have an engineers union. During our latest negotiations the company representative told the union that one of their demands is to reduce our lunch hour from the present forty-two minutes (yes— exactly forty-two minutes— even a buzzer rings)—to thirty minutes. When asked why, the company representative said that it's because not enough people are using the cafeteria—if the lunch hour is only thirty minutes, no one will be able to go out to lunch; therefore they will have to use the cafeteria. It seems that they are losing money!! (By the way, the food really stinks there.)

From: (name withheld)
To: scottadams@aol.com

Scott,

A few weeks ago, I overheard a discussion in the hall about a new, company-wide software QA manual. I listened in and heard it mentioned that the preamble decreed that all employees developing or using software for sensitive work are obliged to conform to the procedures described in the manual. This is essentially everything that I do. Kind of odd that I only found out about it by overhearing a conversation.

So, I head off to the documents people and ask for a copy. The guy there says, "I can't give you a copy of that, it's protected."

"Well, how do I get one?"

"You need this form filled out with all of these managers' signatures."

"But it says right at the front of this document that I am obliged to do what it says, or else!"

He looked up at me suspiciously and asked, "How do you know that?"

I gave up and took a copy of the form.

From: (name withheld)
To: scottadams@aol.com

Scott,

This really happened:

We recently moved into a new building. Since all companies are worried about showing a profit, it's no longer automatic just to order lots of supplies or all of the chairs, cabinets, and things everyone wants. Nothing is ordered if it isn't requested.

Our modular furniture had been delivered and assembled. Shortly after, the "white boards" were delivered and mounted on the walls. At an executive staff meeting the question was asked "Will we be getting board markers and erasers?"

The response from the manager responsible for supplies was,

"Well, I don't think so . . . it seems to me the boards get written on once and then never erased."

After seeing the expression on everyone's face, he added, "Maybe I should rethink that one."

From: (name withheld)
To: scottadams@aol.com

Scott,

One of the things I like most about my current job is that I haven't felt impelled to scream, "I'm living in a Dilbert cartoon!" every five minutes, unlike I was in my previous job.

Well, that was something I used to like. Until now.

I will describe [company] Soda Situation to you in hopes that you'll find something amusing in our misery, something that you can use to torture Dilbert and Wally.

We have until recently been a little startup company. Like most startup companies, our company does everything it can to keep us here working. Continuously. It does its best to make sure we don't leave our desks. It trucks in food, juice, soda, espresso machines, video games, and all the comforts of home. Or it used to, anyway.

The food was the first to go. We were told it was being "evaluated," which is apparently shorthand for "suspended, and we hope you'll forget about it soon and not hassle us." Next, we were told that we'd be charged $3 to get replacement access cards, because "people were 'losing' them too often."

The quotes around "losing" in the e-mail infuriated a lot of people. What, we're losing our cards *on purpose*????? Is there some kind of black market in access cards? Huh?

The free juice and soda seemed unassailable, until now.

We noticed two weeks ago that the refrigerators were looking a little empty. Popular soda types were gone, the milk for the espresso machines was just a distant memory, and the juice bottles were looking pretty scant.

Things continued like this for days, getting slowly worse as people moved on from the good sodas to consume the yucky sodas. Eventually, the fridges were totally emptied, and people started sending e-mail to our facilities people.

This is the answer they got, sent to the whole company, with the name of the culprit deleted:

—————

Hello all:

We are currently going through a cost-cutting "experiment" with coffee, beverages, kitchen supplies, and office supplies. We have temporarily asked our vendors to cut down on our usual weekly inventory.

During this experiment, we hope to determine what kind of beverages and coffee are consumed more than others. We hope to find out what flavors of juices/Calistoga water/sodas we can eliminate, so that we can make sure that we'll never be understocked of those more popular items or overstocked on those that are less popular.

The very same goes for office supplies. We're trying to determine how many different kinds of pens/paper/envelopes/etc. we really need to stock.

We'll continue to order special items that you request. All we ask is to keep the cost down. A $15 Rolodex will do the same as a $50 one. Please use good judgment.

So please bear with us. I will be monitoring both beverage and coffee inventory as well as office supplies during this experiment. If we are low or out of coffee/water/soda/milk/etc., please keep me informed. The same goes for office supplies. In the meantime, please check our other kitchens and supply rooms on other floors to get what you're looking for. It would also be appreciated and beneficial if you would use each product to its fullest. Which means finishing your can of soda before grabbing another one or using some of our used binders before grabbing a new one.

You can also help us by keeping our kitchens and supply rooms clean as you would in your own home.

Thanks for your help. I will inform you as soon as this experiment is complete.

-K

_____

I think the rest of the story should be allowed to tell itself. Here are some responses to that e-mail, and the mysterious K's replies.

___

Reply and response pair one:

___

K:
We're not sure how cutting down on beverage inventory will help determine usage. With reduced inventory our preferred drinks run out and we're forced to consume inferior beverages.

For example, I prefer to drink Coke. The building is now out of Coke, so I drink root beer instead. The problem is, I hate root beer. I drink it only because I need caffeine and root beer is better than any of the other alternatives. However, since I'm drinking root beer, you will think there is a demand for it and will order even more. Furthermore, since I'm drinking root beer more than Coke, you'll think I like it and will order more root beer than Coke in the future.

Yikes!

It seems that an effective way to monitor consumption would be to order large, equal amounts of each beverage, wait a week, and then see how much of each beverage is left.

-T

——-

T:

Excellent point! But, if you are an avid Coke drinker like you say you are, then you'll be willing to go to different floors to find your Coke. I know we have Coke here on the first floor. It's a bit inconvenient, but you may find it to be worth the trip. I myself am an avid Diet Coke drinker. I do like root beer, Mountain Dew, as well as Coke, but I prefer Diet Coke. So I'm willing to check other floors first before I go to my alternate choice. But that's just me.

-K

——-

Reply and response pair two:

——-

K, forgive me for sounding rude, but this is ridiculous. I am not willing to interrupt the important work I'm doing here on the third floor to wander around the other two floors checking to see whether or not there is any of the drink I prefer. Wandering like this is a serious drain on my productivity, and will just make me mad if I don't find what I'm looking for on some other floor. Having some drinks sometimes available on some floors is not a reasonable alternative.

If your goal is to determine which drinks people prefer, then the scheme of ordering fewer of all drinks will definitely lead to skewed results, as T pointed out. People will drink things that are not their preference, simply because their preference is not available.

I have been drinking only apple juice recently. Several times in the last few weeks, there has been no apple juice, so I didn't drink anything and was in a bad mood instead. I'm not sure how this helps your experiment but maybe it's data you want to know.

—J

——-

J:

Thanks for your data!

—K

——

Reply and response pair three:

——-

K:

The shortage of juice is making me very angry. There is no juice at all in the third-floor refrigerator. I don't drink carbonated things, so the Veryfine juice is the only thing provided by the company that I will drink.

Our old ration of juice was already small enough that we usually ran out of juice before the refrigerator got restocked. Now it seems that we have even less juice and we're out even in the morning.

I started eating lunch before noticing the lack of juice. I am very thirsty, annoyed, and have a lot of work to do. I am now going to have to visit all the other floors to find out if there's anything I can drink in the building.

Did you change the drink order to create an artificial shortage? Why?

This is really inconvenient for me!!

—D

——-

D:
>Did you change the drink order to create an artificial shortage?
YES!
>Why?
A DECISION THAT WAS NOT MINE. AGAIN, IT'S ONLY IN
ITS EXPERIMENTAL STAGE AND WILL BE INCREASED
SHORTLY.
   >This is really inconvenient for me!!
I APOLOGIZE. I'M ONLY DOING WHAT I WAS TOLD.
—K

———-

Is K channeling Catbert?
   I think they'd have outraged fewer people if they just started
charging for soda. Meanwhile, we continue to purchase expensive
[equipment] and pay useless employees. I think we should just pay
for the soda by taking just one employee out back and shooting
him/her. I suggested that we choose the employee by a company-
wide vote. Nobody's yet told me I'm insane.

THERE'S HOPE

Last, here's my favorite e-mail message of all time. It gives me hope that
our species has a chance of surviving.

From: (name withheld)
To: scottadams@aol.com

Scott,

When I was younger, I made a trip to Chicago. When I got out of a cab, my umbrella fell on the street and got run over before I could retrieve it. When I submitted my expense report, I put in $15 for my umbrella. Naturally the accountant disallowed it. Next time I put in an expense report, at the bottom I wrote, "Now find the umbrella!"